ICON ENGLISH READING SUCCESS
STAGE II

Icon English Language Training Corporation

Icon English Reading Success: Stage II
Copyright © 2018 by Icon English Language Training Corporation

No part of this publication may be reproduced, distributed, or transmitted in any form or by any means, including photocopying, recording, or other electronic or mechanical methods, without the prior written permission of the author, except in the case of brief quotations embodied in critical reviews and certain other non-commercial uses permitted by copyright law.

Tellwell Talent
www.tellwell.ca

ISBN
978-0-2288-0672-1 (Paperback)

Table of Contents

Introduction vii
Passage 1: Family 1
Passage 2: Soccer Game 5
Passage 3: Father's Day 9
Passage 4: Away Game 13
Passage 5: Campus Visit 17
Passage 6: Paul at the Hospital 21
Passage 7: Ellen's Prom 25
Passage 8: Growing a Garden 29
Passage 9: Career Shadow Day 33
Passage 10: Household Chores 37
Passage 11: Mrs. Martin Teaches Math 41
Passage 12: The Martin Family Visit London 45
Passage 13: Family Dinner 49
Passage 14: College Applications 53
Passage 15: John Goes to a Party 57
Passage 16: Ellen's Social Life 61
Passage 17: Grocery Shopping 65
Passage 18: Outdoor Activities 69
Passage 19: Getting a Dog 73
Passage 20A: Family Reunion 77
Passage 20B: Family Kickball Game 81
Passage 21: Moving Day 85
Passage 22: Paul's Social Life 89
Passage 23: John's Mock Trial at UBC 93

Passage 24: High School Play 97
Passage 25: John and Bella's Date 101
Passage 26: Driving School 105
Passage 27: Summer Job 109
Passage 28: Volunteer Work 113
Passage 29: Building a Résumé 117
Passage 30: Climate Change Project 121
Passage 31: Halloween Party 125
Passage 32: Christmastime 129
Passage 33: Art Class 133
Passage 34: English Test 137
Passage 35: Music Lessons 141
Passage 36: Science Fair 145
Passage 37: PE Class 149
Passage 38: Geography Class 153
Passage 39: First Dance 157
Passage 40: Drama Club 161
Passage 41: Field Trip 165
Passage 42: Valentine's Day 169
Passage 43: Vancouver Aquarium 173
Passage 44: Plagiarism 177
Passage 45: Stanley Park 181
Passage 46: Cooking Class 185
Passage 47: SAT Tutoring 189
Passage 48: Swim Lessons 193
Passage 49: Flying to Boston 197
Passage 50: Family Trip to Boston 201

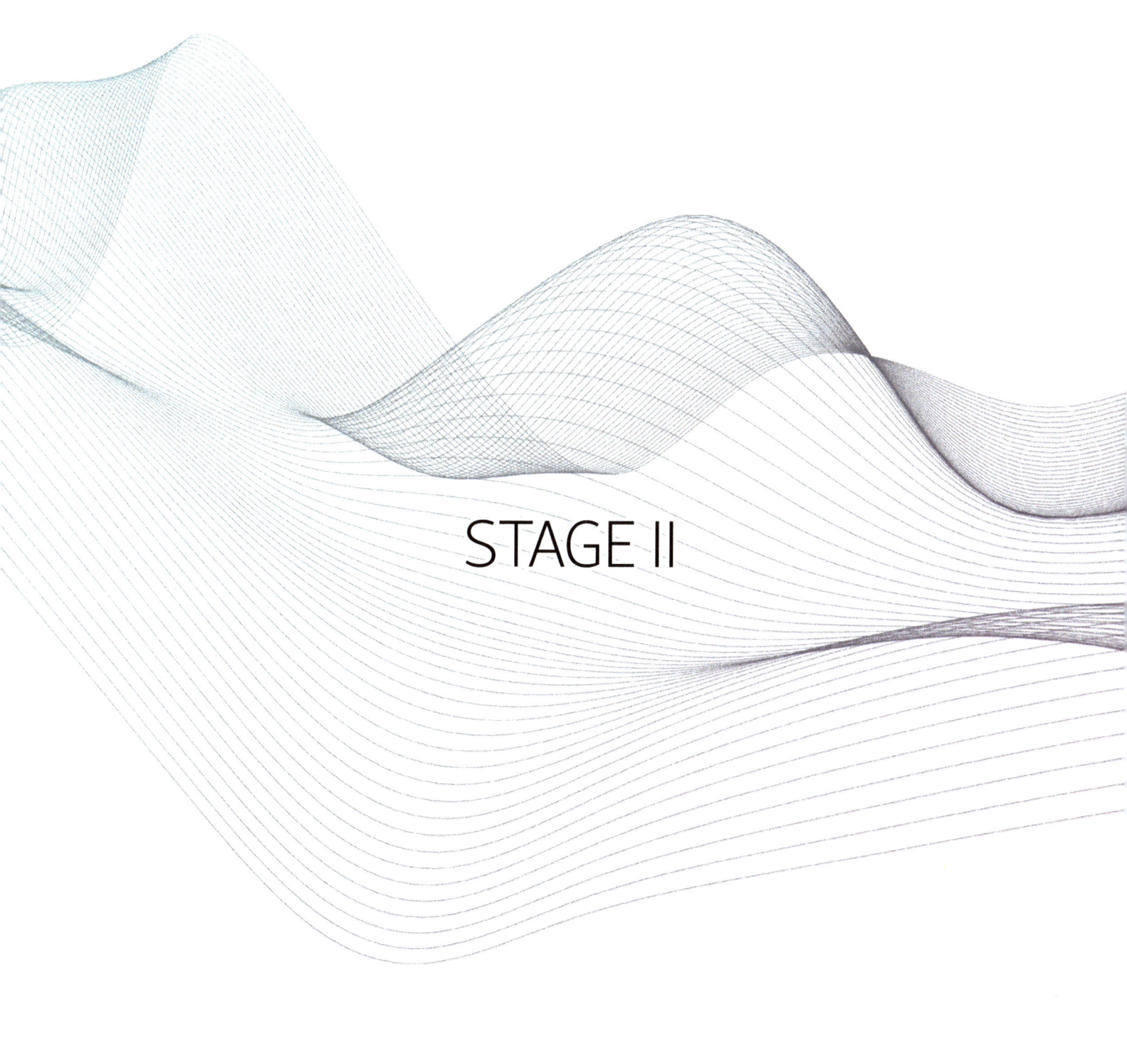

STAGE II

Introduction

The *Icon English Reading Success* is a series of books, each intended for your use when learning English either with a teacher in a classroom or independently.

Learning a new language can be tedious. Sometimes it feels like a chore, and many times people give up before they have even learned the basics. Perhaps, this is due to the fact that many traditional methods of language teaching have become so predictable and monotonous that they're just plain boring. Our books aim to change that.

Within these pages, you'll find something few language books offer: a story. Using the narrative form, our books follow the Martin family through their daily lives. Master the sentence structures and learn new words while following Mr. Martin on an average workday at the hospital. Come to understand various grammar rules as the Martin children do things like learn to play guitar, apply for college, and act in the school play. Grasp strange new tenses like present perfect or future continuous as Mrs. Martin tries to balance her work life with her sometimes-chaotic home life.

While Stages One and Two focus on the Martin family and teach beginner and intermediate reading levels, Stage Three is filled entirely with academic reading passages. In Stage Three, readers will learn about politics, the economy, the environment, and much, much more—all while getting a grasp on complex ideas and more complicated aspects of the English language.

Who is this book aimed at?

Book Two is aimed at intermediate learners who are attempting to improve their English language proficiency level. Besides the basics of English language, such as the past, present and future tense and common verbs, Book Two will delve into more difficult territory and explore compound tenses, words, and more uncommon verbs and adjectives. These books are designed to explain and teach English in a way that even the most inexperienced learners can follow and easily comprehend.

Introduction

How is Icon English Reading Success different from other books?

While many textbooks utilize memorization and repetition as its primary tool for teaching and learning English, *Icon English Reading Success* employs such tactics as narration and context to teach the ins-and-outs of vocabulary, tenses, sentence structure and more. Equipped with an accompanying online learning system, this book can be used for the solo practitioner or for a classroom setting.

Each book also comes with a workbook, designed to enable learners a chance to practice their skills in a challenging but accessible way. As the contents of each chapter grow more advanced, so too will the workbook practice lessons. The effectiveness of each workbook lesson will partly depend on the learner's attention to detail within the textbook lessons, while simultaneously relying on context and practice, rather than memorization.

Icon English Reading Success is designed to be an exciting tool for people of all ages! Our books will not only provide an effective learning experience, but also guarantee that you will achieve learning success while having fun reading them!

Introducing the Martins

Paul Martin— "Hello! My name is Paul Martin. I am the patriarch of the Martin family. I have two daughters and a son. My wife, who I love very much, is Lauren. I have worked as a doctor at the Vancouver General Hospital for nearly twenty years. I enjoy fishing, cooking with my youngest daughter Alice, eating sushi, and being in the outdoors."

Lauren Martin—"Hi there! My name is Lauren. I am the matriarch of the Martin family, and I am the wife of Paul. I work as an elementary school math teacher. I like to go hiking with my husband and teaching is my passion! Oh, and I LOVE autumn. October is hands-down the best time of year!"

Introduction

John Martin—"What's up! My name is John. I am the oldest child of Paul and Lauren Martin. Currently, I'm studying law at the University of British Columbia. I'm also dating a gorgeous girl named Bella. In my free time, I like to go home to visit my parents and two sisters. I recently started playing guitar, and like my father, my love for sushi knows no bounds."

Ellen Martin—"Hey! My name is Ellen. I am the middle child and oldest daughter. I am a senior in high school and I play clarinet in the school band. I love reading the *Harry Potter* books and hanging out with my band friends. In my free time I volunteer at a local animal shelter. And don't tell anyone, but I have a crush on Bella's brother, Cameron... Nice to meet you!"

Alice Martin—"Hiya! I'm Alice, the youngest child. I go to high school with my big sis Ellen, but I'm a freshman. I'm in the drama club and I play soccer too! During the summers I work at a bookstore because like my sis, I love to read. I also enjoy cooking with my dad. Though I can be a bit of a trouble-maker, my family loves me all the same!"

Cameron— "Hello, my name is Cameron! I go to high school with Ellen and Alice Martin, and like Ellen I am in the school band, though I play trumpet and not clarinet. My big sister Bella goes to UBC with Ellen's brother, John, who is also her boyfriend. Oh, and don't tell anyone but I have a bit of a crush on Ellen..."

Bella—"Greetings! I'm Bella. I'm Cameron's big sister and I go to UBC. I'm currently dating John Martin, and I am studying to be a scientist! In my free time I hang out with my roommate. I'm not much of a partier, so I tend to spend my weekends either reading, doing homework, or going on walks. Nice to meet you!"

Icon English Reading Success: Stage II

Passage 1:
Family

There are five people in the Martin family. The **father**'s name is Paul. He is a doctor at Vancouver General Hospital. The **mother**, Lauren, is a teacher. She works at the elementary school. She teaches math. Paul and Lauren have a **son** and two **daughters**. The oldest child, John, goes to college at UBC. He wants to be a lawyer. The youngest child, Alice, is fifteen years old. She is in high school. Alice is on the soccer team. Ellen is the middle child. She is also in high school, and plays clarinet in the school band. Sometimes the band plays at football games.

Ellen has many friends in band. Her best friend's name is Cameron. Cameron plays trumpet. He wants to be a musician. He is the best player in the band. Cameron has a **sister** named Bella who also goes to school at UBC. Bella wants to be a scientist. She has a class with John. They are friends.

The Martins are considered a "**nuclear family**" because they consist of two **parents** and their **children**. They are very **close-knit**. The members of the Martin family eat dinner together every night. Mr. Martin likes to cook, and Alice helps. Bella and Cameron come over for dinner sometimes, but they rarely invite their parents along. Their parents argue often, so Bella and Cameron like to go to the Martin's house for dinner to get away from the noise.

When they come over for dinner, Bella and John usually talk about college. They enjoy the classes, but it is hard work. Mrs. Martin wants to visit her son next week. Ellen asks if she can go too. She agrees but says Ellen must finish her homework. Ellen finishes her dinner and goes to her room. Ellen's English teacher told the class to read fifty pages, so she has a lot of work to do!

Words: father, mother, son, daughter, close-knit, nuclear family, brother, sister, child, parents

Passage 1: Family

Write a summary of the passage using the repeated grammar rules and tenses you can find in the passage. Focus on grammar and tense, NOT story plot points.

_____
_____
_____
_____
_____
_____
_____
_____
_____

Circle all the **nouns**:

Paul and Lauren love their children. John misses his parents but enjoys studying at the university. Ellen hopes she can go to UBC like her brother. Alice is busy with soccer, drama club, and classes at the high school. She isn't sure where she wants to go to university yet.

Place a checkmark (✓) next to the sentences that are correctly written in the **present tense**.

____ Lauren Martin love her children.
____ Paul hopes John will come home soon.
____ Alice and Ellen is sisters.
____ Ellen is in band.
____ John goes to UBC.
____ The Martins is a nuclear families.

Write 2-3 sentences in the **present tense**.

_____
_____
_____

NOTES

NOTES

Passage 2:
Soccer Game

Alice had a **soccer** game on Tuesday. Her mother, Mrs. Martin, asked Alice's sister Ellen to go with her. The game started at 12pm. It was a hot day. Ellen and her mom brought cold drinks to the game and sat under a tree next to the **field**. Alice did not feel well. After the game she became sick. They drove home, and Alice then slept all day. She didn't even bother taking off her soccer **uniform**!

Their father came home from work around 6pm. He checked on Alice. When he came back, he said she would be ok. She was just running a fever. He asked Ellen's mom how the soccer game went. Alice's **team** had **won**. They had won three games that year, and only **lost** once! Mr. Martin was proud of her.

The next day, Alice's teammates came over.

"Is she ok?" asked her friend Jules.

"We miss her!" said Karen.

Mrs. Martin invited them in for a snack. Alice came downstairs to say hello. She was feeling better. They all went into the living room. Alice, Jules, and Karen watched TV together. The mother and father sat on the couch and read the newspaper. Ellen played a video game on her computer and leaned **against** the sofa. After an hour, Jules and Karen had to go. The Martin family said goodbye to them.

Later that night, Alice and Ellen talked about John. They missed their brother very much. They decided to call him. He answered the phone, and all three of them talked until midnight. Their dad came upstairs and **yelled** at them because they were loud. Alice and Ellen said goodnight to John and went to bed.

Words: soccer, yell, uniform, team, goal, win, lose, lost, field, against

Icon English Reading Success: Stage II

Passage 2: Soccer Game

Write a summary of the passage using the repeated grammar rules and tenses that you can find in the passage. Focus on grammar and tense, NOT story plot points.

_____
_____
_____
_____
_____
_____
_____
_____

Circle all the **pronouns** in the following sentences:

He misses his sisters. Alice and Ellen love their brother and they miss him too. Alice said she wants to visit John. Ellen agrees with her. She also wants to visit him.

Write 2-3 sentences in the **past tense** using these verbs: be, run, want, like.

_____
_____
_____

Rewrite the following sentence so that it is in the **past tense**.

I watch TV with my friends and then we go to the park.

_____
_____

NOTES

NOTES

Passage 3: Father's Day

The third Sunday in June is **Father**'s Day. Ellen's dad is a doctor at the **local** hospital. In his free time, he likes to go fishing. Her mom, Mrs. Martin, **decided** to book a small **cabin** near a lake. On the Friday before Father's Day, they will drive to Lake Crescent, which is known for its beautiful **landscape**. They are going to surprise their father with a fishing **trip**! John, the brother, will decorate the cabin. Mrs. Martin called a bakery and ordered a giant cake. Alice and Ellen are going to pick it up. After the Martin family arrives at the cabin, they will go to a fancy dinner. Their dad likes Japanese food, so they are going to a sushi restaurant. John has never eaten sushi. Ellen thinks he will enjoy it.

After dinner, they will go to see a film at the local **cinema**. Mr. Martin wants to see the new Marvel movie. His favorite superhero is Iron Man. Ellen bought him a cool Iron Man shirt for Father's Day. She is excited to **give** it to him. He will love the **gift**! Ellen asked Alice and John what they bought him. Alice got their father a new wallet. John got him a great hat. Their mom will help the kids wrap the gifts. They will give him the gifts after the movie.

The next day, they will all go fishing. Their mother **rented** a big boat. They will drive the boat around the lake. Mrs. Martin is going to give Mr. Martin a brand new fishing rod. They are excited to go to Lake Crescent! Ellen looks forward to seeing her father's surprise. He is going to have a good time.

Words: father, cabin, trip, gift, cinema, give, local, decide, rent, landscape

Icon English Reading Success: Stage II

Passage 3: Father's Day

Write a summary of the passage using the repeated grammar rules and tenses that you can find in the passage. Focus on grammar and tense, NOT story plot points.

_____
_____
_____
_____
_____
_____
_____
_____

Rewrite these sentences so that they are in the **simple future tense**.

Ellen and Alice go fishing with their dad. He is surprised by the trip. This Father's Day is fun.

_____
_____
_____

Circle the **adjectives** in the following sentences:

He drives a fast car. The seats are shiny leather. I said I was very impressed with his driving skills. He was flattered by my sincere compliment. He is happy to drive me to new places. All I have to do is ask politely.

Write a sentence using 2 **adjectives**.

_____

NOTES

NOTES

Passage 4: Away Game

Cameron and Ellen play in the high school band. Last week was their first away **football game** of the year. Ellen thought the game would begin early, but it began at 7pm. They arrived at 6:30 for practice. The band teacher, Mr. Jones, said they would play at 8pm. Ellen felt **nervous**. Luckily, Cameron comforted her. He said it would be fine. They would **probably** not mess up. Afterwards, Mr. Jones said they could walk around until halftime. He said they would need to be back in fifteen minutes.

Ellen assumed they would be given dinner, but she was wrong. She was very **hungry**. Cameron and Ellen eagerly went to the concession stand. Ellen bought a soda and a chocolate bar. Cameron got a **piece** of pizza. Ellen told him pizza might make him sick. Lightheartedly, he ignored her.

At 8pm Mr. Jones announced it was time. There are 4 people who played clarinet in the band, and Ellen was one of them. The clarinet **players** were going to be in the front row. The football team quickly ran off the field. The rival high school band was going to play first. They were truly talented. Ellen looked over at Cameron anxiously. He sat a few seats away and looked really **nervous**. Cameron would play trumpet soon. She smiled encouragingly at him, and he smiled back.

Once the rival band finished their show, Ellen and her bandmates marched gracefully onto the field. Mr. Jones wished them luck. They played their show, and at the final **crescendo**, everyone **clapped** and **cheered**. Everything went perfectly! Cameron and Ellen hugged each other afterwards. They then spent the rest of the evening happily playing music with their band friends.

Words: football, crescendo, probably, cheer, game, players, clap, piece, nervous, hungry

Icon English Reading Success: Stage II

Passage 4: Away Game

Write a summary of the passage using the repeated grammar rules and tenses that you can find in the passage. Focus on grammar and tense, NOT story plot points.

_____
_____
_____
_____
_____
_____
_____
_____

*Circle all the **adverbs** in the following sentences:*

He slammed the door angrily. He was rudely awakened by the rooster calling loudly outside his bedroom. He closed the window quickly and went back to bed. Unfortunately he could not fall back asleep. He begrudgingly got up for the day.

*Write 2-3 sentences in the **past future** tense. Include at least 3 **adverbs**.*

_____
_____
_____

*Place a checkmark (✓) next to the sentences that are written in the **past future** tense.*

____ We would get there by car.
____ I was approaching the door.
____ He was going very fast.
____ She thought they would be there by now.
____ They would arrive around 9pm.
____ We were doing our best.
____ She was not happy with the results.

NOTES

NOTES

Passage 5:

Campus Visit

Ellen and her mother go to visit John at the **University** of British Columbia. John is a second-year **college student** studying law. When they arrive, he takes his sister and mother to lunch at a café on **campus**. They ask if he has been there before. He says he has, but not since September. They all order salads and eat outside. John tells his mom he wants to visit home soon. She asks if he has taken his final exams yet. He told them his midterms would be over in three weeks. He has begun to study for them already!

After lunch, he **guides** them around campus. They stop by the **library**. He has worked there on a group project recently. When they go into the library's study room, he sees his **classmates** are still there. They are surprised to see him—he has been gone only a few hours! He tells them he will see them again soon. On the way out, he tells his mom and sister that he has finished his work for the group project.

Next, Ellen, Mrs. Martin, and John go to John's **apartment**. He has two **roommates**. One of the roommates' names is Ben. Ben is a computer engineer, and he was John's freshman-year **dorm** roommate. Ben recently got a cat. The cat's name is Arnold. Arnold the cat is very friendly, and Mrs. Martin loves him! Mrs. Martin has wanted to get a cat for years.

John's other roommate, Todd, isn't there. Todd has worked at a nearby coffee shop for the past few months. Mrs. Martin has met Todd already. When she helped John move into the apartment, Todd was there to help out. Ellen has not met Todd. Ben asks Mrs. Martin, Ellen, and John if they have gone to go to the art museum. None of them has been there before, so they agree to visit the museum. They all say goodbye to Arnold the cat and leave for the museum.

Words: campus, college, university, library, classmates, students, dorm room/dorm, apartment, roommate, guide

Passage 5: Campus Visit

Write a summary of the passage using the repeated grammar rules and tenses that you can find in the passage.

_____
_____
_____
_____
_____
_____
_____
_____

Write 2-3 sentences in the **present perfect** tense.

_____
_____

Underline the **transitive verb** in the following sentences.

> She plays piano very well and likes to practice after school.
> He painted the canvas in streaks of red and smiled at his masterpiece.
> I want a new book to read for the long flight.
> We ate burgers with cheese and drank big sodas.
> I folded my clothes and put them away.

Rewrite these sentences so that they are in the **present perfect** tense.

> I worked at the bank for two years: _____
>
> Someone ate my soup: _____
>
> I read that book: _____
>
> We took the dog for a walk: _____

NOTES

NOTES

Passage 6:
Paul at the Hospital

Paul got a job at the **hospital** seventeen years ago. He had gone to college at the University of Toronto and graduated in the year 2000. After college, he had briefly worked at a clinic. Six months later, he had started his job at the Vancouver General Hospital. When he began working there, he knew it would be **challenging**.

Recently his daughters, Alice and Ellen, visited him at work. When they arrived at the hospital, Paul greeted them. He showed them around and introduced them to his coworkers, all of whom were **doctors** and **nurses**. Then he took his daughters to the **cafeteria**. Alice had recently gotten food poisoning from an egg sandwich, so she got a hotdog instead. Paul and Ellen got **salads**. They sat at a table outside in the sun.

In the middle of lunch, Paul was called in to see a **patient**. He told his daughters to wait there. The patient was Mrs. Martin! She had accidentally cut her hand while chopping carrots. Paul cleaned the **injury**. Lauren said it hurt, so Paul gave her **medicine**. Then he stitched up the wound. Lauren thanked her husband, and Paul returned to the table outside of the cafeteria. His daughters were still close by, but they had moved to a shaded area under a tree. Ellen had gotten **sunburns** many times before, due to her fair skin. The girls smiled at their father.

"What happened?" asked Alice.

"An older lady had cut herself quite badly," replied Paul.

"Is she ok?" said Ellen.

"She will be fine," said Paul. He smiled **reassuringly**.

Words: doctor, nurse, injury, injured, challenging, medicine, hospital, patient, sunburn, cafeteria, salad, reassuringly

Icon English Reading Success: Stage II

Passage 6: Paul at the Hospital

Write a summary of the passage using the repeated grammar rules and tenses that you can find in the passage.

_____
_____
_____
_____
_____
_____
_____
_____

*Rewrite the following sentences so that they are in the **past perfect** tense:*

I did everything I could: _____

She asks him to join her: _____

They will get food poisoning: _____

We appoint a new leader: _____

They read every book: _____

Transitive or intransitive verb?

The dog ran. _____

I kicked him. _____

She sings beautifully. _____

I ate the last apple. _____

We went to the movies. _____

The light was shining. _____

*Write a sentence in the **past perfect** tense.*

_____

NOTES

NOTES

Passage 7:
Ellen's Prom

Cameron and Ellen had been friends for five years. They met in middle school band class. Cameron liked Ellen, and the high school prom was approaching. He decided to ask her to the **dance**. They had never gone on a **date** before, but Cameron was **confident**. He came up with a plan. During the lunch hour, Cameron went to her locker. He decorated the outside with ribbons and bows, then he taped a note to the locker. It simply said, "Prom?" Cameron hoped Ellen would know he had written it. He didn't want to go to the dance with anyone else.

At the end of the school day, Ellen went to her locker. Cameron was **hiding** behind a door. He waited until she had opened the note and then walked over to her. Ellen looked up and smiled. Cameron smiled back. He handed her a **bouquet** of daisies.

"Will you go to prom with me?" he asked.

"Of course I will!" she said.

Later that week, Ellen was so excited that she went dress shopping with her mother and sister. They looked at countless dresses and went to dozens of stores. Ellen felt discouraged. They had gone shopping three days in a row, but she still did not have a dress. Just as she was giving up on finding a perfect dress, they walked past a **storefront**. In the window was a **beautiful** purple and blue gown.

"You have to try that on!" said Alice, her sister.

"That would look lovely on you," said her mother.

They all went inside the store. Her mother asked an employee if Ellen could try on the **dress** on **display**. The employee led Ellen towards the changing rooms. After Ellen tried on the dress, she came out of the dressing room. Her mother and sister applauded.

"That's the one!" said her mother.

"It's perfect!" said Alice.

Ellen spun around in front of the mirror. She really did look great.

Words: dance, dress, date, confident, excited, beautiful, storefront, display, hide, bouquet

Icon English Reading Success: Stage II

Passage 7: Ellen's Prom

Write a summary of the passage using the repeated grammar rules and tenses that you can find in the passage.

_____
_____
_____
_____
_____
_____
_____
_____

*Underline the **prepositions** in the following sentences.*

I was shocked by his ability to lie.
The bird flew above my head.
The dog ran after the ball.
We went down to the beach.

We hid behind the curtains.
The movie was about race in America.
Ghosts can move through walls.
He is going to the show with us.

*Write 2 sentences in the **present perfect** tense using 2-3 **prepositions**.*

_____
_____

NOTES

NOTES

Passage 8:
Growing a Garden

Alice has always wanted to have a garden. Her mother decided it would be fun. They chose a patch of grass in their backyard that seemed best for growing crops. Then they went to the hardware store. In the back of the store were **garden supplies**. There were all kinds of **plants**. Alice went to the roses. They smelled incredible. Alice wanted to plant some roses, but her mother told her roses are **extremely** difficult to **grow**, and that they should **try** something easier first. Next, they went to the tool section, where they found **shovels**, **soil**, and gardening **gloves**. After that, they were off to the seed section. There must have been a sale earlier that week because there weren't many options to choose from.

An employee came over and asked if they needed help. Mrs. Martin told him that she and Alice were starting a garden, but they didn't know what to grow. Then she asked for suggestions. The man picked up a packet of tomato seeds and handed them to Mrs. Martin.

"I love tomatoes!" said Alice. "Are they hard to grow?"

"Not at all! They will grow very fast," said the man.

"**Amazing**! What about strawberries?" asked Mrs. Martin. Mrs. Martin thought strawberries tasted great, and she didn't think they seemed very difficult to care for. The employee then told her that strawberries are one of the more challenging fruits to grow, especially for beginner gardeners.

"We could use a challenge," said Alice, smiling. She added the **packet** of strawberry seeds to their **shopping cart**.

"How about cucumbers?" said the man.

Mrs. Martin didn't want to admit it, but cucumbers made her burp! It was a **silly** reason not to grow cucumbers, so she kept it to herself and politely said no. The man held up a different pack of seeds.

"How about yellow squash?" he asked.

"We can try!" said Mrs. Martin.

By the end of their shopping spree, Mrs. Martin and Alice were ready to grow strawberries, tomatoes, squash, carrots, peppers, and zucchini. They would have a lot of work to do when they got home!

Words: extremely, packet, shopping cart, plants, garden, supplies, amazing, grow, silly, try, shovel, gloves, soil

Icon English Reading Success: Stage II

Passage 8: Growing a Garden

Write a summary of the passage using the repeated grammar rules and tenses that you can find in the passage.

_____
_____
_____
_____
_____
_____
_____
_____

Circle the **linking verbs**:

> I love cooking spaghetti. Tomatoes are my favorite food and I love the way they taste. Cooking my own meals makes me feel like a responsible adult. I like coming up with interesting meals. But the best part is always tasting the end product! It seems like food tastes better when you put love and passion into the process.

Write 2-3 sentences using the following **linking verbs**: remains, get, appears.

_____
_____
_____

Write a sentence in the **past future** tense using 1 **adverb**.

_____

NOTES

NOTES

Passage 9:
Career Shadow Day

At Ellen's high school, seniors are required to participate in **Career** Shadow Day. Students are asked to find adults and follow them around for a full **workday**. Ellen asked her father if he knew of anyone at the **local newspaper**. She had been considering pursuing **journalism** after **graduating** high school. He spoke with a friend whose niece worked at the newspaper, and they agreed to let Ellen come to the office.

The lady's name was Alyssa Cho. Alyssa had been a journalist at the newspaper for five years. On Career Shadow Day, Ellen arrived at the newspaper **office** at ten o'clock in the morning. Alyssa was waiting outside.

"You must be Ellen," said Alyssa.

"Are you Mrs. Cho?" asked Ellen.

"You can call me Alyssa," she replied. "Please come in so I can show you around."

Everyone at the office was very kind and welcoming. However, Ellen realized she ought to have brought a notebook. If she wanted to be a journalist, she would need to learn how to take notes!

"Could you tell me how you got your job?" asked Ellen.

"I got a **degree** in journalism at UBC," said Alyssa. "If you hope to be a writer, you should do the same!"

Alyssa led Ellen into her office.

"Did you ever write for your high school newspaper?" asked Ellen.

"I didn't, but I wish I had. That might have given me a head start!" said Alyssa. "Do you?"

"No, but I might!" replied Ellen.

"Journalism is a great career path. You ought to try writing for the school newspaper."

"I do want to," said Ellen. "But I'm so busy!"

"You will find time if it's **important enough**," Alyssa told her.

Words: career, journalism, newspaper, degree, important, local, enough, workday, office, graduate

Passage 9: Career Shadow Day

Write a summary of the passage using the repeated grammar rules and tenses that you can find in the passage.

_____
_____
_____
_____
_____
_____
_____
_____

Write a sentence in the **simple future** tense using 1 **pronoun**.

_____

Do these sentences use an **auxiliary verb**? **YES** or **NO**

I am looking for a new job. _____   We bought a used car. _____
John should do better next time. _____   Do you know if he made dinner? _____
We will board the boat. _____   She has done everything. _____
They have decorated the house. _____   I tried to look surprised. _____

Circle all the **auxiliary verbs** in the following sentences:

I am sitting at the table.   He has looked everywhere for the hat.
We should be there.   The cookies are cooling on the counter.
I might be arriving early.   I will do the dishes.

Write a sentence using an **auxiliary verb**.

_____

NOTES

NOTES

Passage 10:
Household Chores

When John was younger, his parents made him and his sisters do **chores every week**. On Tuesdays he would have to sweep every **floor** while his oldest sister Ellen would vacuum the carpets. On Wednesdays, they cleaned the windows. If they finished early, their parents said they could watch **television** for an hour.

But Alice did not like doing chores. She complained about them almost every day. John told her she should just do the chores and be quiet, or else they would all get in trouble. Their father was very **strict** about them doing chores, and John had been punished for not doing them before. He knew that if Alice didn't help out around the house, their dad might take away their allowance.

One day, Ellen and Alice were told to wash all of the bed sheets. Ellen asked her sister if she would rather wash the sheets or fold them once they were dry.

"I don't want to do either," Alice said angrily.

"Neither do I, but we must. Otherwise dad will punish us!"

John came into the room and saw them arguing. "Will you two please get to work? Mom and dad will be home soon! If we don't have the chores finished by the time they come back, he might take away our **allowance** this week!"

"Why do we have to do chores anyway?" Alice **whined**.

"Don't be **childish**," John told her. "If you don't help Ellen with the laundry, I will tell dad you were being disobedient."

"You wouldn't!" Alice cried, shocked.

"I would, and I will. So, get to work or else!" John **threatened**.

Words: television, childish, strict, chores, allowance, week, floor, every, whine, threaten

Write a summary of the passage using the repeated grammar rules and tenses that you can find in the passage.

_____
_____
_____
_____
_____
_____
_____
_____

Write 2 sentences in the **past perfect** tense using 2 **adjectives**.

_____
_____

Do these sentences contain a **modal verb**? **YES** or **NO**

I can speak two languages. _____
May I borrow that book? _____
You biked to work. _____

It will be quicker to travel by train. _____
I can't help you. _____
He wasn't aware of the issue. _____

Write a **question** containing a **modal verb**.

_____

NOTES

NOTES

Passage 11: Mrs. Martin Teaches Math

Mrs. Martin teaches fifth grade at Pear Tree **Elementary**. She has twenty-four students. Her favorite subject to teach is math. Last month she began teaching her students multiplication. Some of them understood the **concepts** very quickly. Others needed extra help. One of her students is named Alex. Alex is eleven years old. He is older than most of the students because he was held back a year for not doing well on the end-of-year tests. At the beginning of the year, Mrs. Martin became **determined** to help him graduate fifth grade so that he could attend sixth grade next year at the middle school with all of his friends. She stays after school to give Alex extra math lessons. Today, she is helping him learn **multiplications** of five.

"What is two times five?" she asks.

"Thirteen?" he says, unsure of himself.

"If you **add** five and five, what do you get?"

"Ten," he answers. She then asks Alex what five times three is. Alex scrunches up his face and thinks for a **moment**. Mrs. Martin catches him silently counting on his fingers.

"Fifteen?" he says.

Mrs. Martin is proud. She asks him how he reached that **conclusion**, and he tells her that he simply added five together three times. Just then, a teacher knocks on the door. Mr. Bailey, the art teacher, comes in. He has just been in the parking lot helping children find their parents' cars. Mr. Bailey tells Alex that his parents are waiting for him. Mrs. Martin looks surprised that it's gotten that late and asks for the time.

"It's a quarter past four o'clock," Mr. Bailey tells her.

Alex wants to know what a quarter means, so Mrs. Martin tells him this: a quarter means one fourth. One quarter of one dollar is twenty-five cents, because there are one hundred cents in a dollar. But one hour is sixty minutes, and one fourth of sixty is fifteen. Alex looks confused by this explanation. He tells Mrs. Martin that he doesn't **understand**, but she laughs.

"Don't worry," she says. "We will learn **division** another day."

Alex grabs his backpack and waves goodbye, and then walks out to the **parking** lot with Mr. Bailey. Mrs. Martin watches them go and smiles. She is sure he will graduate elementary school this year thanks to her extra tutoring and his dedication to learning.

Words: elementary, add, multiply, determined, concept, moment, understand, division, parking, conclusion

Icon English Reading Success: Stage II

Passage 11: Mrs. Martin Teaches Math

Write a summary of the passage using the repeated grammar rules and tenses that you can find in the passage.

_____
_____
_____
_____
_____
_____
_____
_____

*Write out the **number**:*

2: _____ 84: _____
11: _____ 19: _____
4: _____ 63: _____

*Write the **year**:*

Two-thousand fourteen: _____ Nineteen eighty-six: _____
Eighteen forty-three: _____ Seventeen seventy-six: _____

*Write the number **or** symbol:*

One plus four is: _____ Sixteen minus two is: _____
Four times two is: _____ Seven plus nine is: _____

NOTES

NOTES

Passage 12:
The Martin Family Visit London

Mr. and Mrs. Martin had been wanting to go on vacation for a very long time. Their jobs were stressful and **demanding**, and they needed a break. Summers were often too busy for **travel**. They decided to take their two daughters, Alice and Ellen, and their son, John, along with them. The kids had been well behaved lately, and school had just let out for Christmas break. Mrs. Martin had always wanted to travel to London; her husband had been there only once before, but he wanted to return.

The kids were **thrilled**. Mr. Martin booked hotel rooms, everyone packed their bags, and they all headed to the **airport**. The flight from Vancouver to London was extremely long—close to ten hours! When they landed in London, it was early morning. The Martin family were all **jet-lagged**. They went straight to the hotel. When they got there, the hotel lobby was packed! They waited in line for thirty minutes before one of the hotel **receptionists** was available. When a spot finally opened up, Mr. Martin asked why it was so busy.

"You came in December! What did you **expect**?" said the **rude** receptionist. "Winter is busy enough, but it's even more crowded in the summer."

Mrs. Martin loved fall, and always wanted to go to London during October or November. In her opinion, autumn was the best season, and she loved to imagine all of the beautiful fall colors against the English backdrop: all of the leaves changing from green to red and yellow, orange pumpkins, and of course plenty of **rain**! When Mrs. Martin mentioned this, the receptionist snapped at her, saying they had plenty of rain as it is.

John approached the counter. "You don't have to be mean."

The receptionist sighed and apologized and then asked Mr. Martin for his date of birth to confirm their reservation. Mr. Martin recited his birthday, and the receptionist typed it in. Then he gave them their room key, and once again apologized to the family for his rudeness, citing stress as his reason.

"It's quite all right," said Mrs. Martin. "We'll have to come again in fall or spring when it's less busy!"

"October, November, March and April are the best months to visit," said the receptionist. "But be warned—April is always our rainiest month!"

Words: airport, travel, jet-lagged, thrilled, rain, receptionist, expect, rude, demand

Icon English Reading Success: *Stage II*

Passage 12: The Martin Family Visit London

Write a summary of the passage using the repeated grammar rules and tenses that you can find in the passage.

_____
_____
_____
_____
_____
_____
_____
_____

*Write 2-3 sentences in the **future tense** about your favorite holiday.*

_____
_____
_____

Complete the date for each holiday:

Halloween: 31st of _____ (month)
Christmas: 25th of _____
New Year's Day: 1st of _____
US Independence Day: 4th of _____
Your birthday: _____ of _____
April Fool's Day: 1st of _____

Name the four seasons:

_____   _____
_____   _____

NOTES

NOTES

Passage 13:
Family Dinner

Every evening Ellen's family eat **dinner** together around six o'clock. Sometimes cooking takes longer than usual, so occasionally they will eat later. Last Wednesday, Mr. Martin made fried **chicken**. Alice helped him in the kitchen, and he showed her how to make it. First, the chicken was covered in **flour** and spices, then it was cooked in a pan with oil until it turned crispy. Alice and her dad loved to make **food**, and everything they cooked was **delicious**. As a result, they cooked dinner for the rest of the family most nights. However, they always made sure to cook dinner on Fridays and Mondays because on these days Mrs. Martin worked late.

Around six-thirty, the table was set with silverware and plates, and Ellen went around pouring drinks for everyone. Alice had milk, Ellen had water, and their parents both drank wine. Although John was still away at college, they had gotten used to his **absence**. Suddenly in the middle of dinner, just as Mrs. Martin was about to take her first **bite**, Alice reached for the **bread** and **accidentally** bumped her mother's arm. Mrs. Martin's fork dropped to the ground. There was a silence, and Alice thought everyone would yell at her. Instead, they all burst out laughing; Alice was pretty clumsy, but they quickly cleaned it up and went back to enjoying their home-cooked meal. They discussed school, Alice's upcoming soccer games on Saturday and Sunday, Ellen's college applications which were due next Tuesday, and their parents' days at work. Around seven o'clock they **cleaned** up dinner, and Ellen and Alice went upstairs to finish homework. The house was dark and quiet; everyone was asleep by eleven o'clock that night.

Words: accident, clean, bite, delicious, bread, chicken, dinner, food, flour, absence

Passage 13: Family Dinner

Write a summary of the passage using the repeated grammar rules and tenses that you can find in the passage.

_____
_____
_____
_____
_____
_____
_____
_____

Write a sentence using a **semicolon**.

_____

Write today's date:

(day number) _____ (month) _____ (year) _____
Which day comes after Thursday? _____
Which day follows Sunday? _____
What day of the week is it today? _____

Write 2-3 sentences in the **future tense** using at least 1 **comma** and 1 **adverb**.

_____
_____
_____

NOTES

NOTES

Passage 14:
College Applications

Ellen had three more university **applications** to fill out. She knew that her college essay had to be better than other applicants her age, so she spent an entire week writing it. She made it as **honest** and well written as she could— she knew she would have to **impress** the people reading it and make it the best essay of them all! Her English teacher, Mr. Allen, had read over her essay and had offered pointers on how to improve it. His input had been very **helpful**. She liked him more than most of the other teachers at school because he always demonstrated true dedication to his students. His input practically **guaranteed** an acceptance to one of the colleges!

Ellen had completed five college applications already; those applications had been much less difficult and the least stressful. But in her opinion, it was all worth it; she really wanted to go to college–more than any of her friends. Her brother John had told her that college was a great opportunity to **network** with **professionals**. He told her that the classes were much more difficult than high school classes though, so she would have to work hardest at keeping her **grades** up. Ellen was prepared. She knew that no matter which school **accepted** her, she would try her best. Now all she had left to do was pick a **major**!

She loved reading and she loved playing music in the band, but Ellen thought teaching would be the most sensible option. She considered journalism too; however in her opinion, journalism was a less interesting profession to her than teaching. The wisest advice she got from her teachers was this: take a few classes outside your comfort zone, and see what you find the most interesting!

Words: professional, application, accept, helpful, guarantee, honest, impress, grade, major, network

Passage 14: College Applications

Write a summary of the passage using the repeated grammar rules and tenses that you can find in the passage.

_____
_____
_____
_____
_____
_____
_____
_____

Complete each sentence using a **superlative**.

We have the _____ dog in the world!
This homework is the _____ assignment our teacher has ever given us!
That book was the _____ book I've read all year.
My mom is the _____ mom in the world.

Write 2-3 sentences using **comparatives**.

Example: Her sweater is warmer than mine.

_____
_____
_____

NOTES

NOTES

Passage 15: John Goes to a Party

John's first college party was tonight. He was anxious because he had been told that most college parties were **wild**, so he decided to go with his roommate, Todd. The party would be at a **fraternity** house on campus, and it started around ten o'clock at night. John wasn't sure what to expect. Regardless, he knew Todd would insist on doing something fun that night, and that was ok with him—most nights he only watched TV and went to bed early! This would be a welcome change. Besides, Todd would refuse to do anything else that night, so John didn't have much of a choice!

When they got to the frat house, the party was already **underway**. People were standing around outside, and inside the crowd was **rowdy**. Getting inside was **strenuous** because of how crowded it was. The lawn out front was littered with **trash**: discarded plastic cups, cigarette butts, confetti, and food wrappers. It was a **mess**. There were even people sitting on the **roof**! Todd and John glanced at each other. They silently agreed to do as little damage as possible to the already very messy house.

John found his biology classmate Andrew in the kitchen. They liked biology because it was a difficult subject. They agreed, however, that they often procrastinated finishing their homework because of how hard it could be. Todd also told Andrew that he wouldn't mind doing some extracurricular activities in his free time.

Only an hour or two **later**, police arrived to shut the party down! Apparently, neighboring apartment complexes were complaining about the noise. These neighbors had called the **police** because they thought doing so might intimidate the party-goers into being quieter. The police showed up, and then John and Todd said goodbye to Andrew before calling a cab to take them back to their apartment.

Words: underway, fraternity, strenuous, rowdy, wild, later, mess, trash, police, roof

Icon English Reading Success: *Stage II*

Write a summary of the passage using the repeated grammar rules and tenses that you can find in the passage.

_____
_____
_____
_____
_____
_____
_____
_____

Do these verbs need to be followed by a **gerund** (verb-ing), **infinitive** (to verb), or **either** (both are correct)? Try coming up with sentences in your head to see which one sounds right.

Remember: Stop:
Wait: Plan:
Volunteer: Suggest:
Go: Begin:
Prefer:

Are these sentences **correct** or **incorrect**?

He expects to winning the game. _____
I wouldn't mind going with you. _____
She dislikes to run in the rain. _____
We can't afford to go on vacation. _____
I pretended to being sick. _____
Ben couldn't imagine living without his dog. _____

Rewrite the incorrect sentences from above so that they are correct:

_____
_____
_____
_____
_____

NOTES

NOTES

Passage 16:
Ellen's Social Life

Ellen wanted her friends to go with her to the **mall** last weekend. Her **best friend**, Alyssa, asked Ellen to pick her up from her house because Ellen had a driver's license. They met their other friends, Jen and Mark, at the mall. Mark had brought along his younger brother, Ben. Ben was an **acquaintance** whom Ellen knew because he was in her sister's class. Mark told them that he wanted to cheer his brother up, and that bringing Ben to the mall with them was a **no-brainer**.

The group went first to the department store, where they spent an hour trying on clothes and modeling sunglasses for each other, all the while laughing and joking around. But Ben seemed like he was in a bad **mood**. Ellen asked Mark to go to a different section, so she could talk to him. Once they were out of earshot, she **glanced** at Ben from afar and asked Mark if his brother was ok. Mark said he wasn't sure. Ellen decided to talk to Ben herself.

"Is everything ok?" she asked him. To her surprise, Ben confided to her that he had **failed** his math test, to which she responded, "It's ok. I've failed tests too."

"I stopped my dad seeing the grade by hiding the test," said Ben. "But I know he'll find out sooner or later."

Ellen told Ben not to worry and said that her mom could probably give Ben extra math tutoring if he needed. "My mom will help you learn the math concepts in no time!"

Ben looked up. He had a smile on his face. "You think so?" he asked.

Ellen grinned. "Absolutely! The tutoring will prevent you from doing badly on a future test! I'm sure of it."

Words: mall, best friend, acquaintance, no-brainer, mood, glace, fail, grin

Icon English Reading Success: Stage II

Passage 16: Ellen's Social Life

Write a summary of the passage using the repeated grammar rules and tenses that you can find in the passage.

_____
_____
_____
_____
_____
_____
_____
_____

*Put a checkmark by the sentences that **correctly** use the **verb + object + infinitive + gerund** format:*

I didn't want the dog to start barking. _____
The homework will help you to improve your skills. _____
We are going to be leaving soon. _____
Eric asked Laura to go swimming with him. _____
The students wanted to sit by their friends. _____

*Write 2-3 sentences that uses the **verb + object + infinitive + gerund** format:*

_____
_____
_____

Passage 16: Ellen's Social Life

NOTES

NOTES

Passage 17: Grocery Shopping

Mrs. Martin and Alice were on the way to the **grocery** store. That night, Mrs. Martin would be making her eldest daughter Ellen some spaghetti, one of Ellen's favorite dinners, as a way of congratulating Ellen on doing so well on her recent test. Alice had come along to help. When they got there, they saw a big puddle on the floor of one of the **aisles**. A sign had been put up on either end to block the aisle, to prevent any customers from slipping on the floor before it was properly cleaned. Alice left to grab the potato chips while Mrs. Martin went over to the meat section. A recent news article had warned meat-eaters against buying ground **beef** due to a recent E. coli bacteria **breakout**, so Mrs. Martin instead bought chicken.

Meanwhile, Alice stood in the pasta aisle looking at the various kinds of noodles. To her right, she saw a man put his hand into his coat pocket and then shoot her a nervous glance. It looked like he might have put something into his pocket. Alice suspected the man of stealing, but she hadn't seen enough to convict him. She didn't want to accuse him of taking something if he hadn't actually done anything wrong, so she kept her mouth shut. Alice grabbed two boxes of pasta noodles and sauce, then hurried back to her mother.

Mrs. Martin thanked Alice for grabbing the sauce from the next aisle over. She was glad Alice would be helping her cook because her husband would not be able to help with dinner that night. He was going to be working late. She felt bad that she rarely cooked dinner, but Mr. Martin had forgiven her because he knew she was busy with teaching and cooking could be very **time-consuming**.

As Alice and Mrs. Martin headed for the checkout line, she noticed Alice had grabbed two bags of **generic brand** potato chips. Mrs. Martin asked Alice why she did not take Lay's, and Alice said she'd like to save some money. As they were unloading their groceries from their **cart** into their car in the parking lot, they heard the store alarm go off. Alice watched as a store employee handcuffed the man who was indeed a **shoplifter**. She had been right all along!

Words: grocery, aisle, beef, breakout, time-consuming, generic, brand, cart, shoplifter

Passage 17: Grocery Shopping

Write a summary of the passage using the repeated grammar rules and tenses that you can find in the passage.

_____
_____
_____
_____
_____
_____
_____
_____

Write a sentence in the **verb + object + preposition + gerund** format using these verb/preposition combinations:

Example: Thank... for: We thanked him for giving us the time.
Stop... from: _____
Talk to... about: _____
Prevent... from: _____
Suspect... of: _____

Correct these sentences so that they are in the **adjective + infinitive** format:

I was eager hearing about my grandfather's war stories:

_____

She is content playing piano all day:

_____

They are happy doing all the work:

_____

The school was excited hosting the event:

_____

Our city is perfect visiting during the summer:

_____

NOTES

NOTES

Passage 18:
Outdoor Activities

Paul Martin and his wife, Lauren, love the outdoors, so they are going **hiking**. They choose a place to go hiking, get in their car, and head towards the **park**. The park is on the **outskirts** of town, but it is a national park, so in their opinion, it's worth the drive. When they arrive, they leave their car in the gravel lot, grab their water bottles from the backseat, and head towards the **map**. A park ranger is standing next to it. His job is to make sure people take care of the land and don't disrupt the **wildlife**. As they are approaching the park ranger, he waves to them.

"Good morning!" says Lauren.

"Hello!" replies the park ranger. "What **trails** are you two going on today?"

"We aren't sure," says Paul truthfully. "We haven't been to this park in many years. Can you **suggest** one?"

They all look at the map. The ranger points to a **specific** trail. "This path is perfect for new hikers."

"But we aren't new hikers," says Lauren.

The ranger points to another path. "Well then this one might be better. It is going to be a long hike up the mountain, and you might be **exhausted** once it's over, but the view from the top is worth the trek!"

Lauren and Paul thank the **ranger**, and then they start walking towards the path. Just as they are beginning to walk out of sight, the ranger calls out to them: "Be **careful** of **snakes**!"

Lauren gives Paul a worried look. Her eyes are growing wider. She is wondering if they'll see a snake on their hikes. She is terrified of them! Paul can sense her fear. He is trying not to laugh at the concerned look on her face. Instead, he pulls her close and holds her hand. When he looks at her again, she is smiling. She isn't looking too concerned about wild snakes anymore!

Words: hike, ranger, trail, exhausted, suggest, park, snakes, careful, map, specific, wildlife, outskirts

Passage 18: Outdoor Activities

Write a summary of the passage using the repeated grammar rules and tenses that you can find in the passage.

_____

_____

_____

_____

_____

*Rewrite these sentences so that they are in the **present-continuous** tense:*

They go to the amusement park:

_____

I studied for the test:

_____

She acts afraid of the spider:

_____

He runs this morning:

_____

I left my hat behind:

_____

*Write 2-3 sentences in the **present-continuous** tense.*

_____

_____

_____

*Place a checkmark (✓) next to the sentences that are in the **present tense** and a star (*) next to the sentences that are in the **present continuous** tense.*

___ We are trekking back to the campsite.
___ I am trying my hand at skateboarding today!
___ They are tired after the marathon.
___ I am losing my mind.

___ Dawn is approaching.
___ It is interesting to say the least.
___ We are sick of the hot weather.
___ He's starting to fall in love with you.

NOTES

NOTES

Passage 19:
Getting a Dog

Finally, the Martins decided they were going to get a **pet** dog. Ellen and Alice had bothered both of their parents about it for years. Mr. Martin didn't want a dog because he knew how much care they required. Mrs. Martin didn't want one because the dog would shed hair all over the place, and already she was anticipating having to clean up after it! But Ellen and Alice pleaded and begged, so their parents eventually caved. Besides, Alice had just won the lead role for the high school play, so they figured a **reward** was in order!

The four of them drove to the animal **shelter** and then looked at all of the dogs. A small Labrador immediately caught Alice and Ellen's attention; they bee-lined it for the cage. The dog was wagging its **tail**. He was brown with **unique** white markings all over, and he was whining quietly, as though begging to be let out to play. One of the animal shelter **employees** came over to them.

"Do you want to pet him?" she asked.

Alice and Ellen nodded their heads. The woman picked up the dog and led them into a private room, and the Martin family followed her inside. As soon as the lady set the dog down, it began sniffing around the room. Alice and Ellen were stroking its back lovingly.

"Dogs make great **companions**," said the lady. "And this one has a lot of **personality**!"

"Can we get him?" asked Alice, pleading with her eyes.

"Not unless you're going to take full **responsibility** for it," said Mr. Martin.

"We will! We swear!" said Ellen. The dog **settled** down between the girls and began to doze off.

Mrs. Martin wrapped her hand around her husband's arm. She was smiling at him. Mr. Martin rolled his eyes and then laughed good-naturedly. The girls were looking at him expectantly.

"All right, fine! But I'm not cleaning up after it!" he exclaimed.

Words: pet, companion, responsibility, tail, employee, unique, personality, reward, settle, shelter

Icon English Reading Success: Stage II

Passage 19: Getting a Dog

Write a summary of the passage using the repeated grammar rules and tenses that you can find in the passage.

_____
_____
_____
_____
_____
_____
_____
_____

*Put a star next to the sentences that are written in the **past continuous** tense:*

They were looking for a new apartment. _____
The teacher was annoyed with the students. _____
Were you listening closely? _____
I felt increasingly tired and fed-up. _____
How much was it going to cost them? _____
He said everything must go. _____

*Write 2-3 sentences in the **past continuous** tense:*

_____
_____
_____

Past *(P) or* **past continuous** *(PC)?*

I was hoping to see you before you left. _____   We were ready to go home. _____
Was he trying his hardest? _____   I was interested in hearing more. _____
The dog was barking all night. _____   Were you in class for the test? _____

NOTES

NOTES

Passage 20A:
Family Reunion

The Martin family will be going to a family **reunion** this week. On Wednesday they will drive down to Portland, Oregon to visit Mrs. Martin's side of the family. The Martin family is very **large**; Mrs. Martin has five brothers and one sister, so the family reunions are always big events. Mrs. Martin's mother called the day earlier to let her daughter know that everyone will be **participating** in a family kickball game. She said they will choose their teammates when they get there, and **mentioned** that Mrs. Martin's brother is on his city's kickball **league**, so he is a good person to team up with.

The drive down is going to be long, so Ellen packed two different books. If she finishes one of them on the drive down, she will have another to read on the **return** trip! Alice doesn't want to go to the family reunion. Alice told her mom and dad that she would **prefer** to stay at home with their new dog, but Mr. Martin told her that she doesn't have a choice; she will be going to Portland with the rest of the family.

During the drive down to Portland, Mrs. Martin talked to her kids about the weekend plans for the family reunion.

"On Friday we will be competing in the kickball game," she told them.

"But what if I don't want to?" Alice whined.

"All of your **cousins** will be there! It will be fun, I promise!"

That seemed to cheer Alice up a little, but she was **nevertheless** fussy for the rest of the drive. Once they got to their grandmother's house, all of Mrs. Martin's brothers and sisters helped them unload their car.

"You are so going to lose tomorrow!" their Uncle Tim playfully taunted.

"Not if I can help it!" Mrs. Martin replied, and then she pulled out a box from the trunk of the car and opened it. Inside were homemade **jerseys** that Mrs. Martin had made for her husband, Ellen, and Alice. Each jersey had their names across the back and numbers showing their ages.

"You made us jerseys?" said Alice, grinning.

"You bet! We are going to win that game tomorrow," Mrs. Martin said, winking.

(To be continued)

Words: reunion, participate, large, jersey, league, cousin, return, mention, nevertheless, prefer

Passage 20A: Family Reunion

Write a summary of the passage using the repeated grammar rules and tenses that you can find in the passage.

_____
_____
_____
_____
_____
_____
_____
_____

*Put a checkmark (✓) next to sentences that are written in the **future continuous** tense.*

_____ My parents will be coming home soon.
_____ The dog was running away from the cat!
_____ The director will be answering questions about her film.
_____ Are they going to be serving dinner?
_____ Your friends will be worried about you.
_____ I am going to faint.

*Write a **question** in the **future continuous** tense.*

_____

Future (F) or **future continuous** (FC)?

_____ She is going to the orientation.
_____ I will talk to you soon.
_____ Will you be participating?
_____ Lane will be watching the movie with you.
_____ They are going to wait for the signal.

_____ Will you be riding with them to school?
_____ Our pets are going to love the new treats.
_____ I will be eating dinner early tonight.
_____ She will be a great author one day.
_____ Will you be arriving anytime soon?

NOTES

NOTES

Passage 20B: Family Kickball Game

On Friday morning, the Martin family ate a big breakfast. They knew they were going to need a lot of energy to play **kickball** that day. The first match was the Martins against Mrs. Martin's brother Tim's family, the Dolmans. Tim Dolman had one daughter named Nancy, who was going to be turning fourteen in a few weeks, and two sons named Dustin and Lucas. Dustin was twelve, and Lucas was thirteen. Tim's wife, Mrs. Martin's sister-in-law, was named Carol.

"This game is going to be **insane**!" said Nancy to Alice.

Mr. Martin **overheard** the two girls talking and said to Nancy, "I hope you guys bring your game face because we will be playing our hardest! Isn't that right, Alice?"

Alice rolled her eyes. "Whatever you say, Dad!"

The game began at ten o'clock. Mrs. Martin's other **siblings** and parents were **gathered** on either side of the big field. The game would be timed for thirty minutes. Whoever had the most points at the end of those thirty minutes was going to be playing the next team.

The sun was bright, and the game was **thrilling**. At the end of the thirty minutes, the Dolmans had won, much to Mr. and Mrs. Martin's surprise. Everyone was a good sport, though. The point of the game was not which family was going to be reigning champion, but instead that everyone have fun and spend time together. The day went on, and finally after three matches, the Dolmans won the **competition**.

"It will be **time** to eat lunch soon," Mrs. Martin's mother, Alma, said. "Everyone get cleaned up! We will have lunch ready in an hour."

Everyone headed to their **campers** to shower, tired but happy.

Words: kickball, insane, overhear, sibling, gather, time, thrilling, competition, camper

Passage 20B: Family Kickball Game

Write a summary of the passage using the repeated grammar rules and tenses that you can find in the passage.

_____
_____
_____
_____
_____
_____
_____
_____

Put a checkmark (✓) next to sentences that are written in the **future continuous** tense and a star (*) by the sentences written in the **future tense**.

____ Will you come with me?
____ Lunch will be ready soon.
____ He will be turning 15 this month.
____ I am going to the mall on Wednesday.

____ She will be attending the party tonight.
____ The book is going to be a huge success
____ Will you be helping me with dinner?
____ Are you going to be waiting all night?

Write 2-3 sentences in the **future continuous** tense.

_____
_____
_____

NOTES

NOTES

Passage 21:
Moving Day

In a month, the Martin family would be moving into a new house. Alice and Ellen began **packing** their rooms up two weeks in advance because they knew that the earlier they began packing, the easier the move would be. The day before they were going to move out of their house, Mrs. Martin checked the weather. She hoped it would not be raining tomorrow, but she told everyone they should be wearing raincoats just in case.

The next morning, they woke up around eight o'clock. The moving **truck** arrived at ten o'clock, and they began putting **boxes** in the back. Around **midday**, Alice asked if they would be getting lunch later. Mr. Martin told her not to worry, and that they would start looking for something to eat once everything was packed. Mrs. Martin used a marker to **organize** the boxes so that when they unloaded them into their new house, it would be easier to figure out where each box was supposed to go.

"Do you know if the house will be unlocked once we arrive?" Mr. Martin asked his wife.

"It should be," she replied.

Around midday, Mr. and Mrs. Martin decided they would go get lunch for everyone. Ellen and Alice were **exhausted** from **carrying** around boxes all day, and their parents knew they would not keep working if they didn't have a **chance** to rest. Mr. Martin told his wife to wait there with their daughters, and that he would be returning shortly with food. When he got back, he handed out their sandwiches.

"Shouldn't this sandwich be hot?" Alice asked, biting into hers.

"I asked them to toast the sandwiches, so it should be," said Mr. Martin.

"Can I microwave mine?" asked Alice. "It's not hot **anymore**."

Mrs. Martin pointed at the truck. "The microwave is already packed up. We would have to start opening up all those boxes to find it."

"**Forget** about it; it's ok," Alice said, and began to eat her sandwich.

They ate quickly, knowing they would still have a lot of work to do once they arrived at their new house.

Words: organize, boxes, exhausted, carry, pack, midday, anymore, truck, forget, chance

Passage 21: Moving Day

Write a summary of the passage using the repeated grammar rules and tenses that you can find in the passage.

_____
_____
_____
_____
_____
_____
_____
_____
_____

Write a sentence in the **future continuous** tense.

_____

Write a sentence in the **past continuous** tense.

_____

Write a sentence in the **past future continuous** tense.

_____

Past continuous (PC), **future continuous** (FC), or **past-future continuous** (PFC)?

____ They would be searching for their dog. ____ I was looking for answers.
____ My aunt should be arriving soon. ____ The cops will be asking all of the questions.
____ Would you be working together? ____ It should be snowing again by morning.
____ We will be painting the nursery tomorrow. ____ Alice was reading outside yesterday.

Underline the parts of the passage below that use the **past-future continuous** tense.

A snowstorm was fast approaching and my parents knew that we would be getting close to a foot of snow by the next morning! She tasked my dad with getting groceries but what she didn't realize was this: everyone would be going to the grocery store right before the storm hit! There was mounting hysteria in the grocery store and my dad tried to be patient as he gathered supplies. He knew that we would be thanking him for his patience.

NOTES

NOTES

Passage 22:
Paul's Social Life

Paul's old medical school friend, Tom, is in town. Tom used to live in Vancouver, but for the last three years he has been living in Seattle, so he hasn't seen Paul in a long time. Tom drives to Paul's house, and the two **hug**.

"How was the trip?" he asks.

"I'm exhausted," says Tom. "I have been driving for hours!"

Paul invites Tom inside. They sit in the kitchen for a while **catching up**. Paul asks Tom how long he has been working at the Seattle Hospital, and Tom tells him he has been working there for just over two years, and that he has been enjoying the work.

"It has been rewarding," Tom tells him. "I've seen many of my sickest patients make full recoveries! Anyway, are you hungry? I have been thinking about burritos for the last few hours-- I'm starving!"

The two take a **bus** into the **city** and go to a Mexican **restaurant**. It is one of Paul's favorite restaurants in town. He has been going there once a week for the past three months, ever since the restaurant opened! As they sit down to eat their lunch, Tom **leans** forward.

"So, have you been watching any of the hockey games?"

Paul admits that he has been working so much **lately** that he doesn't have time to watch television. They discuss hockey for a while, and then Paul asks Tom about his wife.

"Actually, we haven't been talking much lately," Tom admits. "She wants a **divorce**."

Paul expresses his **condolences**, but Tom says he is to blame because he should have been paying better attention to his wife and family. Instead, he has been focusing too much on his job. After they finish their lunch, they begin walking towards the movie theater. A new horror movie came out a few days ago, and it has been playing in the theater for the past few days. Paul asks Tom if he wants to go see it. Tom nods **enthusiastically**. He tells Paul that he has been watching a lot of horror movies lately, and that he's been wanting to see that particular **scary** movie for months!

"Let's watch it!" says Paul.

Words: catching up, bus, city, restaurant, rarely, lean, divorce, scary, hug, condolences, enthusiastic

Icon English Reading Success: *Stage II*

Passage 22: Paul's Social Life

Write a summary of the passage using the repeated grammar rules and tenses that you can find in the passage.

_____
_____
_____
_____
_____
_____
_____
_____

Present (P) *or* **present-perfect continuous** (PPC)?

____ *You have been wanting to read that book for years!*
____ *She will escort you to the soiree.*
____ *I practice piano every day*
____ *Have you been watching the TV show?*
____ *She has been asking about you.*
____ *I am lucky to have such a sweet cat.*
____ *He is going for a bike ride.*
____ *She has been singing professionally for years.*
____ *Have you been paying attention?*
____ *I love my new haircut.*

Write a sentence in the **present-perfect continuous** tense.

_____

Write a **question** in the **present-perfect continuous** tense.

_____

NOTES

NOTES

Passage 23:

John's Mock Trial at UBC

John had been preparing for his mock trial for over a month. His professor told the class that they would each have to participate, and he had given each student a role. John was the defending **lawyer**, and as such, he would have to **present** a case declaring the innocence of the **defendant**. For weeks, John had been working on a great opening statement for the case. Over the weekend, he had been trying to make sure the statement was perfect; as a result, he had re-written it multiple times.

The mock **trial** case was simple: the defendant had supposedly been robbing a gas station when he was arrested. However, prior to his arrest, he hadn't been hurting anyone. It had been a simple armed robbery without any **casualties**.

On the day of the mock trial, the students gathered in one of UBC's law classrooms. Everyone had been looking forward to the mock trial for a long time. The students had been talking about it for months, ever since the beginning of term, and now finally it had begun!

John took his seat at a table next to the defendant, another student named Jake whom he had been hanging out with lately, and who had become his close friend. Jake was excited to be playing the role of the defendant, and he had been **practicing** what to say when questioned.

The **prosecutor**, another one of John's classmates named Karen, started giving her opening **remarks** when everyone arrived. She declared that what Jake did was **illegal**. Their professor played the role of the **judge**, and after Karen was finished with her opening remarks, it was John's turn.

He presented his case to the jury, explaining how Jake deserved a second chance and **minimal** jail time. John told the jury that Jake hadn't been hurting anyone during the robbery. At the end of the mock trial, John won the case. Jake was found guilty, but his jail sentence was reduced from fifteen to ten years. The mock trial had been a learning experience; throughout the trial, everyone in the class had been gaining valuable knowledge of how trials would work in a real-life setting!

Words: lawyer, practice, present, remark, prosecutor, defendant, judge, trial, illegal, casualty, minimal

Passage 23: John's Mock Trial at UBC

Write a summary of the passage using the repeated grammar rules and tenses that you can find in the passage.

_____
_____
_____
_____
_____
_____
_____
_____

*Underline the parts of the passage below that are written in the **past perfect continuous** tense.*

I had been steadily losing weight for the past three months when I finally decided to go see my doctor. At first she congratulated me on my figure but then she realized that I had been hoping to gain weight, not lose it! I was becoming dangerously thin. Eventually we found the root of the problem: I had been exercising too much and not eating enough carbs! She told me to take it easy and give my body a rest, and to eat more fatty foods to counteract the intense cardio. I'm glad I went to see her because I had been feeling worried about my sudden, drastic weight loss!

Identify the tense: **past-future continuous** *(PFC),* **present-perfect continuous** *(PPC), or* **past-perfect continuous** *(PastPC).*

____ We would be baking all day. ____ I have been doing homework for three hours!
____ Dad has been acting strange lately. ____ Would you be driving with us?
____ She had been working too much. ____ Have you been exercising?
____ Should he be doing that? ____ Tara had been studying law at Harvard.

*Write a sentence in the **past-perfect continuous** tense.*

_____

*Write a sentence in the **present-perfect continuous** tense.*

_____

*Write a sentence in the **past-future continuous** tense.*

_____

NOTES

NOTES

Passage 24: High School Play

Alice had won the lead role in the high school play. On Friday night, her sister Ellen and her parents went to see the play. Ellen left earlier than her parents to hang out with Alice before the play.

"After tonight, how long will it have been since you last **performed** in a high school play?" Ellen asked.

"Only one year. I took a year off to focus on soccer," Alice explained. "But after tonight, I will have been in four different plays!"

Ellen was impressed. She had never been in a play before; she was too shy and had **stage fright**. She checked her watch.

"When are mom and dad getting here?" Alice asked. "The play starts in twenty minutes."

"I bet they're already here," said Ellen. "They will have left early to get good seats."

One of the other students in the play came over to Alice to let her know that the rest of the **actors** and **actresses** were getting dressed and putting on makeup.

"You only need twenty minutes to prepare?" asked Ellen, surprised. "I would have thought you needed more time."

"By the time you go to find your seat next to mom and dad, I will have finished putting on my **costume**," said Alice. "It really doesn't take very long!"

Ellen hugged her sister and wished her luck, and then went to find her mom and dad. They were sitting in the fourth row; coming to the play early had been a great idea because their seats were perfect! As they waited for the performance to begin, props were rolled out on stage. Cameron, Ellen's friend, was part of the stage **crew**, and in fact held the title of stage **director**! He had been staying after school to help paint the **props** every day for three months, and she knew he would have done his best to make the props **colorful** and believable. Ellen borrowed her mom's **pamphlet** that had been passed out to the audience, and read about Cameron's accomplishments as part of stage director. The play they were about to see would have been his tenth **production** that he has been part of, and he was only seventeen years old!

Words: actress, actor, stage fright, colorful, director, crew, props, perform, costume, production, pamphlet

Icon English Reading Success: Stage II

Passage 24: High School Play

Write a summary of the passage using the repeated grammar rules and tenses that you can find in the passage.

_____
_____
_____
_____
_____
_____
_____
_____

Future perfect *(FP)* or **past-future perfect** *(PFP)?*

_____ I will have read the entire twelve-book series by the end of this year.
_____ He would have cooked a bigger dinner if he knew you were coming.
_____ We will have been married for 15 years this October.
_____ I would have come sooner had my car not gotten a flat tire.
_____ Would you have said that if you knew the truth?
_____ The president will have been in office for six weeks.

Write a **question** *in the* **future perfect** *tense.*

_____

Write a **question** *in the* **past-future perfect** *tense.*

_____

NOTES

NOTES

Passage 25:
John and Bella's Date

John finally got the courage to ask Bella on a **date**. He knew if he didn't do something, he would regret it, so last Thursday after biology class he asked her to dinner. Around seven o'clock that night, John arrived at Bella's house. He went to the front door and rang the **doorbell**. Bella's roommate, Jess, came to the door.

"You must be John!" said Jess. "You know, if you hadn't asked Bella to go to dinner with you tonight, she probably would have been doing nothing. She likes to spend her Friday nights at home relaxing."

"Hi Jess," said John **awkwardly**. "Do you know if she's almost ready?"

Jess shrugged. "She's been doing her makeup for the last hour. I don't know why it takes her so long!"

John entered their apartment and sat in the living room with Jess while they waited for Bella. When she finally came out, she looked beautiful. Bella was wearing a red dress with black heels. John blushed; he realized he should have been wearing something nicer. After all, this was their first date, and first impressions are important!

As they drove to the restaurant, **silence** filled the car. John knew he should have been asking her about her family, or her other classes, but he was really nervous. And, as Bella's roommate had said, had he not asked her out to dinner, Bella would have been **hanging out** at home, maybe even doing homework. 'Maybe she prefers doing homework and staying in more than she likes going on dates,' he thought.

They got to the restaurant where they had a **reservation**, and the **waiter** came around to take their order. John got a hamburger and beer, but he wondered if he should have been eating healthier that night because Bella ordered a salad and sparkling water. Once the waiter left, John asked Bella how her classes were going.

"Not bad," Bella told him. "However, I went for a **hike** with Jess the other day when I should have been studying for that biology test! I think I **failed**."

"I can help you study," said John.

Bella smiled. "I would like that."

Words: awkward, doorbell, hike, fail, silence, hang out, date, waiter, reservation

Icon English Reading Success: Stage II

Passage 25: John and Bella's Date

Write a summary of the passage using the repeated grammar rules and tenses that you can find in the passage.

_____
_____
_____
_____
_____
_____
_____
_____

*Rewrite these sentences so that they are in the **past-future perfect continuous** tense.*

I made pancakes for breakfast: _____
She exercised yesterday. _____
He was shopping at the mall. _____
My mom was reading last night. _____

*Rewrite these sentences so that they are in the **past-future perfect** tense.*

I should go to sleep.

_____

He helped me with the project.

_____

My teacher gave me a passing grade.

_____

The film won the award.

_____

NOTES

NOTES

Passage 26:
Driving School

A law was passed two years ago requiring new **drivers** to attend driving school. Alice has just turned sixteen, and knows that in order to get a **license**, a test has to be taken after driving classes are over. However, the test was revised by teachers a few months ago, and Alice was told about the revision only a week ago, so she has to find a newer workbook to study. Their new house is being decorated, so she walks a few blocks to a nearby café for some peace and quiet.

Alice gets a coffee and then begins to study in a **secure** corner. The book was written by the driving teacher himself, so she knows she has to memorize everything. The first rule in the book is about **respecting** other drivers. A **successful** driver is one who drives cautiously. Driving the speed limit is **imperative** because going too fast can be **dangerous**. It is better to drive below or right at the **speed** limit; **otherwise**, you can get a speeding ticket from a police officer.

After reading a few chapters, Alice goes home. The test is to be taken the next morning, and her father agrees to drive her there.

"Back in my day, driving lessons were given to teenagers by their parents!" he tells her. "Times have changed."

"I wish I could have taken lessons from you," says Alice. "I would be a lot less nervous!"

The next day, Alice takes the driving test. She is asked by the teacher to demonstrate parallel parking, which she has never done before. As a result, she does not do well. But the teacher is understanding. He tells her to go home, practice parallel parking, and come back the next day. Alice is discouraged, but she remembers her father always tells her that not all problems can be solved by studying. Some problems require a hands-on approach.

Words: driver, imperative, license, otherwise, respect, regular, secure, speed, dangerous, success, successful

Passage 26: Driving School

Write a summary of the passage using the repeated grammar rules and tenses that you can find in the passage.

_____
_____
_____
_____
_____
_____
_____
_____

Write a sentence using the **passive voice**.

_____

Place a checkmark next to the sentences that are written in the **passive voice**.

_____ The table was cleaned.
_____ The real punchline to the joke was my friend's shocked face!
_____ I went to school with him.
_____ The sea was darkened by the storm.
_____ That car belongs to me.
_____ The plants are watered by gardeners.
_____ My journal was written in by me.

Underline the sentences in the passage below that are written in the **passive voice**.

A book report that was written by me was praised by my teacher. She said it was the best book report she had ever read! Flattery and pride was what I felt. The fact that a good grade was given to me was just a bonus! I was overjoyed when she asked if she could keep my book report for future classes. A template would be made by the teacher that would show students how to write an exemplary book report, just like mine!

NOTES

NOTES

Passage 27:
Summer Job

Alice is looking for a summer job. School is finished for the year, and she is hoping to find work **within** the first week of summer vacation. Her mother is helping her apply to **various** jobs by driving her around town every day. Alice has applied to three jobs already, and on Monday she is going to a job interview at an ice cream shop. The ice cream shop is being renovated at the moment, so instead she and her mom go to a bookstore that day.

Today, Alice is applying for a **cashier** job at a **bookstore**. When Alice goes inside, she asks an employee if the **manager** is around. The employee tells her the manager is occupied by another customer at the moment, and then asks Alice what kind of assistance she needs.

"I am looking for work," Alice replies. "Are you hiring?"

The employee shrugs, and tells her the boss is being seen by another customer. Alice browses the store, and just as she is thinking of giving up, the boss approaches her. He is a tall man in his late forties, with **curly** brown hair and **thick glasses**.

"Hi there! An employee told me you were wanting to speak with me?" he says inquisitively.

Alice introduces herself, as does the manager, whose name is Jacob. Alice tells Jacob that she is looking for a summer job, and that she would love to work at the bookstore. Jacob walks over to the customer service desk to give her an application, then asks whether she has ever worked in a bookstore before. Alice tells him she hasn't, but promises that she is going to do a great job if he chooses to hire her. Alice thanks him for his time and goes back to her mother's car with the job application in hand. Her mother is in the driver's seat, and when Alice gets in she sees that her mother is busy with her makeup. Her mother prefers it being **fixed** very carefully using a tissue.

"How did it go?" her mother asks, putting the tissue away.

"Pretty well," says Alice. She explains how the manager gave her the application to fill out, and that he was a very nice person. Her mother asks where they should go next for Alice's job search, but Alice grins.

"I'm thinking we might not need to go **anywhere** else!" says Alice. "I think I have a good chance of being hired!"

Words: fixing, manager, curly, thick, cashier, bookstore, glasses, various, within, anywhere

Passage 27: Summer Job

Write a summary of the passage using the repeated grammar rules and tenses that you can find in the passage.

_____
_____
_____
_____
_____
_____
_____
_____

*Write a **sentence** in the **past continuous** tense.*

_____

*Write a **sentence** in the **present continuous** tense.*

_____

*Write a **question** in the **future continuous** tense.*

_____

NOTES

NOTES

Passage 28: Volunteer Work

After Ellen's junior year of high school, she decided it was time to find **volunteer** work. She had never done any volunteer work, but that only made her more interested in giving it a shot. She knew that whichever **organization** accepted her as a volunteer would be lucky—she was a hard worker! She didn't know where she would end up volunteering, but she needed to start volunteering someplace as soon as possible! Ellen wasn't sure which volunteer work was best for her, so she asked her friend Cameron.

Cameron told her about a **wonderful non-profit** animal **rescue** centre that operated in Burnaby. Ellen drove to the animal rescue centre and met with a woman named Liz. Liz had been working at the rescue centre for fifteen years. That she had been there so long only proved to Ellen how rewarding the work had to be. Still, Ellen admitted that she was worried the volunteer job wouldn't be a good fit for her, but Liz understood. Liz told her to come by the next day to work with them for a few hours to see if she might enjoy volunteering there. The next day, Ellen got to the rescue centre early so Liz could show her around. Liz had not mentioned whether Ellen should dress informally or formally for her first volunteer shift. Ellen hadn't been sure what to wear, so she was dressed casually and hoped it would be **appropriate work-wear**.

Ellen was curious about where Liz had learned so much about animals, so while Liz showed Ellen around the **facility**, Ellen asked Liz about her **background**.

"How long have you known that you wanted to work with animals?" she asked.

Liz shrugged. "I can't remember exactly when I first realized it, but I was young!"

By the end of Ellen's volunteer shift, she was tired, but happy and satisfied with her patience. She knew how she could care for all kinds of injured animals and what she could do to nurse those **malnourished** ones back to health. She knew the rescue centre was a place at which she would enjoy working!

Words: wonderful, organization, background, appropriate, malnourished, non-profit, volunteer, rescue, facility, work-wear

Passage 28: Volunteer Work

Write a summary of the passage using the repeated grammar rules and tenses that you can find in the passage.

_____
_____
_____
_____
_____
_____
_____

Place a checkmark next to the sentences containing a **noun clause used as a direct object**.

____ Do you know who made the cake?
____ His brother is my best friend.
____ Her coworker is angry with whoever keeps parking in his space.
____ The kid denied stealing the cookie.
____ My laptop is what I bring to every class.
____ He didn't mention whether his daughter was coming to the party.

Write your own sentence using a **noun clause** that functions as a **direct object**.

_____

Underline the **noun clause**s in each sentence.

She can't decide which outfit looks best on her.
My brother wants to talk to whoever is in charge.
Can you remember where they want to eat tonight?
Do you know what the weather will be like tomorrow?

NOTES

NOTES

Passage 29:
Building a Résumé

Alice was quickly learning the **importance** of résumés. After landing her first job at the local bookstore, she realized that she would need to **develop** a résumé for future jobs. The problem was that she didn't have much job **experience**. Ellen, her older sister, told Alice that she would help her out with her résumé. Ellen's résumé was great, owing to the fact that Ellen had more job and volunteer experience. Alice had only just begun her first job, and she had never done any volunteer work before, so the question was whether or not her résumé would be good enough for future **endeavours**.

Ellen said to first begin writing down her previous **education**, or which schools Alice had attended. Next, she could write down all of the jobs that she had worked. Alice's résumé was short, but Ellen told her it would be fine. Ellen showed Alice her own résumé, which Ellen had made for her college applications. She told Alice that the **objective** of building a résumé was to show future employers and schools how valuable your work was. If a résumé looked especially **outstanding**, **opportunities** would be **endless**.

One of Alice's biggest concerns was whether or not employers and future colleges would find her application impressive. Ellen reassured her that she still had time to get more experience to put on her résumé, which would be helpful when applying to colleges in a few years. The best college applications were those that had multiple skill sets, jobs, and educational backgrounds listed. But, Alice was not encouraged. She felt she didn't have much to **brag** about. So far, her only crowning achievement at school was that she won the lead role in the school play. She knew that for this lack of achievements, she only had herself to blame. Her excuse for not having more accomplishments was that she was already busy with school, drama club, and soccer.

One of the other issues with her résumé was that unlike her sister, Alice had never volunteered anywhere. Ellen's suggestion was that Alice try volunteering someplace soon. In the end, Alice was worried that her résumé wouldn't be impressive, but Ellen assured her that with more experience, her résumé was sure to improve.

Words: develop, education, experience, importance, endeavour, objective, opportunity, outstanding, endless, brag

Passage 29: Building a Résumé

Write a summary of the passage using the repeated grammar rules and tenses that you can find in the passage.

_____
_____
_____
_____
_____
_____
_____
_____

Underline the **noun clauses** *in the following sentences.*

The test was what she was concerned about the most.
Elsie's problem was that she didn't try hard enough.
His insecurity is what keeps him from meeting people.
My dedication is what helped me win the competition.

Write your own sentence that uses a **noun clause** *as a* **subject complement**.

_____

Place a checkmark next to the sentences that contain a **noun clause** *functioning as a* **subject complement**.

____ I'm curious about whether or not the sun will come out today.
____ The trophy is what makes the marathon worth the effort.
____ What she lacks is genuine motivation.
____ His biggest achievement was winning the Nobel Prize.

NOTES

NOTES

Passage 30:
Climate Change Project

The senior ecology class had been assigned a school **project**, and Ellen had been tasked with the subject of climate change. It was almost unavoidable that Ellen was feeling a little nervous. However, that she was completely prepared was no surprise. Ellen had been closely following the effects of climate change both on the news and online. The fact that her school had even been teaching climate change in the first place was **proof** of how **progressive** it was. It was obvious how the climate changed over the last 100 years, but why climate changed so drastically was a mystery. It is extremely hard, if not impossible, to carry out **experiments** on global climate and get reliable **results**. Ellen decided a **diagram** would be the best way of teaching the effects of climate change on the Arctic. However long it may take, Ellen was determined to make her project the best in the class. Ellen's father promised he would help her build her diagram. Whether or not it turned out well was entirely up to Ellen, however.

They began by sketching a very big picture of the Earth as the **background**, then attaching pieces of white fabric, which would **represent** sheets of Arctic ice. Above the picture of the Earth was a light bulb, which would represent the sun. Whenever the bulb got brighter, little pieces of the fabric would break off from the larger piece. Whichever pieces of fabric that she colored blue would in turn represent melted ice.

On the day she was to present her project, Ellen decided last minute to include an **informational** video. What the video discussed were the numerous, **substantial**, and deeply negative effects of climate change. Whatever the students paid attention to, they were sure to understand climate change by the time she was finished with the presentation. The teacher asked which student would like to present first, but no one raised a hand. Everyone was nervous, so he decided to try something different. Whoever presented first would be given five extra points on their project. With that, at least ten students raised their hands, all of them now eager to present first.

Two students presented before Ellen, and after Ellen presented hers, the class applauded! What the teacher gave Ellen after her presentation showed Ellen that even her teacher might have learned something new from her presentation because the teacher gave her an A+!

Words: project, experiment, progressive, result, informational, proof, substantial, represent, background, diagram

Passage 30: Climate Change Project

Write a summary of the passage using the repeated grammar rules and tenses that you can find in the passage.

_____
_____
_____
_____
_____
_____
_____
_____

Write a sentence that use a **noun clause** as:

1.) Subject complement: _____

2.) Subject: _____

Does this **noun clause** act as a **subject** (S) or **subject complement** (SC)?

____ She isn't sure whether or not her sister is mad at her.
____ Whoever leaves last has to stack the chairs and sweep the restaurant.
____ I told her that I didn't know how to solve all her problems.
____ What they regretted most was not going on a honeymoon after the wedding.
____ The people who graffitied the bathroom stall were probably drunk.
____ The issue is that you never stop to think before you speak.
____ What they didn't expect was that I might arrive to the surprise party a few minutes early.

Passage 30: Climate Change Project

NOTES

NOTES

Passage 31:
Halloween Party

Halloween was approaching, and Mr. and Mrs. Martin wanted to throw a party. It was their favorite holiday, and they had begun planning for the party two months in advance. The holiday had roots in the pagan festival called Samhain, and the idea that all things spooky can be celebrated was very popular with many children, but Ellen didn't much like Halloween. Her parents, who dressed up every year, **embarrassed** her with their weird **costumes**, so every Halloween Ellen went over to Cameron's house. This year, however, they asked Ellen and Alice to help. Even John was coming home for the holiday! The news that he was coming home made Ellen happy, and she agreed to help out with the party. However, her parents' claim that their house was the best Halloween-decorated house in town really made her feel a little uneasy.

The decorations that the Martin family normally stored in the attic were brought out, and everyone got to work. Ellen hung fake cobwebs in the windows while John put up string-lights. Alice, who often complained when she was told do anything, was happily **carving** a pumpkin in the kitchen. Ellen hadn't had much confidence in the plan that they could finish decorating the entire house by eight o'clock that night. But, it turned out everything was done properly. The living room, which was usually **occupied** with **furniture**, coffee tables and a television, now contained multiple pumpkins, a bowl of fruit punch, a cauldron filled with candy, and skeletons hanging from the **ceiling**. Three witch dolls were placed in various locations around the house. The dolls, which were **battery**-powered, **emitted** high-pitched cackles whenever someone passed by. The ultimate surprise that Mr. Martin had even gone so far as to buy a fog **machine** shocked but excited everyone! The Martin house had come to resemble a haunted house!

Words: Halloween, costume, emit, occupy, ceiling, furniture, carve, embarrassed, machine, battery

Write a summary of the passage using the repeated grammar rules and tenses that you can find in the passage.

_____
_____
_____
_____
_____
_____
_____
_____

Write your own sentence that uses a **noun clause** as a **noun complement**.

_____

Place a checkmark next to the sentences that correctly use a **noun clause** as a **noun complement**.

____ What Alicia said made her friends laugh.
____ What made her late for class was that she forgot to set a morning alarm.
____ The problem with his new phone was that it didn't hold a charge.
____ Her excuse for not reading the book was that it bored her.
____ The graceful, effortless way the dancer moved was what ultimately won her the gold medal.
____ My problem with the movie is that it doesn't have as much detail as the book.
____ Dad's issue with his new physical trainer is that the trainer spends more time admiring his own reflection than actually training him!

NOTES

NOTES

Passage 32:
Christmastime

Now that fall was over, the Christmas decorations were finally coming out of the attic. Because Christmas was Alice's favorite time of year, she wanted to help everyone in the family get in the Christmas mood by putting up winter decorations. Before they put them up, however, the old autumn **décor** had to be taken down.

But Mrs. Martin was upset that autumn had come and gone so quickly; it was her favorite time of year. While Alice was excited for the Christmas **season**, Mrs. Martin usually **mourned** the ending of October and November. All of the leaves had fallen off the trees, and the days were growing shorter and colder. Alice had said it would snow by the beginning of December, and she had been right. On December 7th, it snowed nearly six inches in Vancouver in just one night!

The next day, Ellen made hot **chocolate** for everyone and passed around the mugs while Alice and Mrs. Martin got to work putting up Christmas decorations. They wanted to make sure the house looked especially merry because everyone in the family would be coming over for their Christmas party later that month. As far as she knew, this would be the first time all of their family would be coming to the Martin family's house for Christmas. Usually, Mrs. Martin's brother or her mother and father hosted the **annual** Christmas parties. But since they had moved into a new house, everyone had been bugging Mrs. Martin whether they could come and see it. She had **relented**, and, as a result, she was actually beginning to look forward to Christmas.

Once the roads had been cleared of snow, Alice, Ellen, Mr. and Mrs. Martin went Christmas shopping. Mrs. Martin took Ellen over to the nearby café because they were **distributing** free samples of their seasonal **beverages**—peppermint-flavored coffee! She also wanted to **distract** Ellen while Mr. Martin and Alice went to the music store. Because Ellen had been asking for a new clarinet for years, her parents had decided to buy her one this Christmas.

Words: season, mourn, distribute, chocolate, relent, annual, distract, décor, beverage

Passage 32: Christmastime

Write a summary of the passage using the repeated grammar rules and tenses that you can find in the passage.

_____
_____
_____
_____
_____
_____
_____
_____

True or False?

_____ Adverb clauses modify a verb, adverb, or adjective.
_____ Adverb clauses always contain a subject and an adjective.

Write a sentence containing **adverb clauses**.

_____

Underline the **adverb clauses** *in the following sentences.*

He gives clothes away when they no longer fit him.
She donated her glasses because she didn't like the style anymore.
I made Italian food for the dinner party because that's what my guests like best.
She drove south until she ran out of gas.
We left our boots outside, where they wouldn't track mud over the carpets.
I brought an umbrella because I didn't want to get caught in the rain.

NOTES

NOTES

Passage 33:
Art Class

Ever since she was young, Alice had wanted to learn how to **paint**. She had **enrolled** in her high school art class in hopes that it might improve her **artistic abilities**. Ellen had taken the class before her and had encouraged her sister to give the class a shot. On the first day of class, Alice took a seat next to a girl named Hannah, whom she knew from math class. What she did not know, however, was how talented a painter Hannah already was.

Their teacher, Mrs. Mac, went around distributing **canvases** to each student. She then gave them a lesson on the **fundamentals** of painting, and only after the lecture was over did she allow them to begin to paint. Mrs. Mac urged the students to **sketch** their drawings out before adding color, so Alice obeyed. But Hannah had already begun painting, and it was as if she had been painting her entire life. Alice was amazed. Because of Hannah's skill, Alice herself was nervous to begin painting. She knew she wasn't nearly as talented as Hannah. As Mrs. Mac went around to each table to check on the students' progress, she noticed Alice sitting still, not yet working.

"Is everything ok?" she asked Alice.

Alice nodded towards Hannah, who was painting her **masterpiece**. "I'll never be that good," she said.

"And unless you practice, you'll never **improve**."

Hannah looked up from her painting and smiled at Alice. "I'm only this good at painting because of all the years I've spent practicing!" she explained. "I was a terrible painter at first. It just takes time."

"You see?" said Mrs. Mac. "If you never try painting anything, you'll never be good. You just have to start!"

Alice picked up her pencil and finally began sketching out a landscape. Whether she liked it or not, she knew that Mrs. Mac and Hannah were right. All she needed to do was get started, for one cannot succeed if one never tries!

Words: paint, canvas, artistic, pencil, sketch, ability, fundamental, improve, enroll, masterpiece

Passage 33: Art Class

Write a summary of the passage using the repeated grammar rules and tenses that you can find in the passage.

_____
_____
_____
_____
_____
_____
_____
_____

True or False?

____ Adverb clauses often begin with a subordinating conjunction, such as if, because, in order to, and although.

____ An adverb clause alone cannot express a complete thought.

Write 2 sentences containing **adverb clauses**.

_____
_____

Underline the **adverb clauses** in the following sentences:

He studied until his eyes stopped focusing on the page.
The birds fly South once the weather turns cold.
His laptop is in the car, where he left it last night.
She eats a lot of pasta because that's all she knows how to make.
I picked him up from the airport because I was already close.
The cat ran away when he glimpsed a hungry coyote.

NOTES

NOTES

Passage 34:
English Test

Ellen was very unprepared for her **literature** test. Her English teacher had assigned the class *Pride and Prejudice* to read, which was written by an English **author**. It had been a difficult book to read, which was why Ellen had skimmed over most of it. Because of this, she was **dreading** the test; she knew she would not do well. Students who read the book closely were guaranteed to score well on the **exam**, and Ellen had not done so. This was because the book, which most people enjoyed, had been very boring in Ellen's opinion.

Their teacher, who was addressed as Miss Kate rather than Mrs., had never married, so most of the boys in class had a crush on her. However, this didn't prevent Miss Kate from giving them an extremely hard test. She walked around, **monitoring** the students to make sure none of them were cheating, which had become a problem in the class.

Ellen tried to concentrate on her test, but the boy sitting next to her was clicking his pen. The constant clicking was just one reason why Ellen hated sitting next to him. The other reason was that he often tried to cheat off her tests, but that would be useless today; Ellen was sure she would fail, not to mention the fact that Miss Kate was very **vigilant**.

To her surprise, she was able to answer most of the questions correctly on the first page, which had all been about the author, Jane Austen. Ellen had **researched** the author prior to the exam, so she knew most of the answers. But on the following pages came questions about **chapters** which Ellen had skipped reading. She tried to remember what she could about the end of the **novel**, which was not much.

Within the first ten minutes, a few students had already begun handing in their tests. Ellen decided that people who finished the test this early had considered the test either too easy or too difficult to even attempt to finish. With just five minutes before the class would end, Ellen handed her test over to Miss Kate. The test, which had been even more difficult than she had anticipated, was a lesson to her: do the homework and read the material. If you do so, you won't fail!

Words: literature, novel, author, chapter, exam, dread, vigilant, monitor, research

Passage 34: English Test

Write a summary of the passage using the repeated grammar rules and tenses that you can find in the passage.

_____
_____
_____
_____
_____
_____
_____
_____

Write a sentence containing an **adjective clause.**

_____

Underline the **adjective clauses** in each sentence.

I'm going to visit the house that I grew up in.
The bad weather is the reason why I drove instead of walking to the store.
Do you recall that time when we got lost in the woods?
John, who is Ellen's brother, has never taken a professional music class.
Klarissa is the friend I trust the most.
The house, which the Martin family lived in for 10 years, is finally up for sale again.

NOTES

NOTES

Passage 35: Music Lessons

John's college classes, which had been wearing on him, were always over by five o'clock in the evening, so he decided to take up music lessons. The only problem was that he didn't know what instrument to learn! Todd, his roommate, told him he should try **piano**, but Bella, his girlfriend, said that **guitar** would suit him better. He found an ad, which had been in the school library, for someone offering to give inexpensive music lessons, so John had called the number listed on the ad and set up a time to meet them.

The student was a young man named Walt, which was short for Walter. Walt was in the music program at UBC, and played a **multitude** of **instruments**. Walt's favorite instrument to play happened to be guitar, which was lucky for John. On Thursday, Walt and John met in one of the university music practice rooms. John had rented a guitar from a local music store, and Walt first taught John basic music **theory**. He also gave John a book on music theory, which would be **immensely** helpful to John later on.

First, Walt taught John how to play **scales**, which were a series of notes played on various strings of the guitar. Without knowing notes, John couldn't hope to learn how to play a **melody**, which was his goal. Walt also gave John a short lesson on **rhythm**, and told him how to count measures. People who could correctly count measures would later be able to **identify** time **signatures**, and one concept could not be grasped without the other. At the end of the lesson, which had lasted nearly two hours, John thanked Walt and told him how much he had enjoyed it. Walt, who had never tried teaching music before, blushed, and told him it had been an honor. They set a time for their next meeting the following week, and then **departed**. John left the music practice room humming his favorite **tune**, and was excited to go home, where he would practice the material Walt had given him to study.

Words: melody, multitude, rhythm, instrument, tune, guitar, piano, scale, immense, signature, identify, depart

Icon English Reading Success: Stage II

Passage 35: Music Lessons

Write a summary of the passage using the repeated grammar rules and tenses that you can find in the passage.

_____
_____
_____
_____
_____
_____
_____
_____

*Write a sentence containing an **adjective clause**.*

_____

*Underline the **adjective clauses** in each sentence.*

The library, which is home to thousands of books, is my favorite place to go on Sundays.
The professor that I like the most teaches creative writing.
My car, which has never failed me, finally broke down today.
Her dog, who is a Border Collie-Rottweiler mix, is very friendly.
I wrote a poem which was published in a quarterly arts magazine.
These shoes, which I have had for six years, are finally getting too worn to wear.

NOTES

NOTES

Passage 36:

Science Fair

The high school science fair was approaching, which inspired Alice to make a presentation on **radios**. She had always loved listening to the radio, but it was only recently that she had become interested in the science behind it. She decided to take an **academic** approach to her project, which was considered **extra-curricular**. She would not be graded for the project; she was simply doing it for fun! The **primary** reason she wanted to participate in the science fair was that some of her friends, most of whom were science-minded people, would be **attending**. The **secondary** reason was that she knew her participation would look good on her résumé, which Ellen had recently helped her create.

One of the **remarkable** things about radio was its ability to **broadcast signals** across miles upon miles of land, which sparked a **revolution** in communication and prompted a wave of radio stations to come into being. NPR, which was based in Washington, D.C., was her favorite station to listen to. The people who reported for NPR always had the most **soothing** voices, and at night they played classical music, which helped Alice fall asleep. For the project, she chose to create her very own radio station. This proved more difficult than she imagined. For starters, she would have to obtain a licence to broadcast anything, a licence which could only be obtained through the FCC, or the Federal Communications Commission. And in order to get a licence from the FCC, she would have to take an examination. It was after finding this out that she understood why radio was so regulated; many of the adult programs were restricted to certain late-night hours, and this prevented less mature audiences from hearing anything inappropriate.

In the end, Alice wasn't able to take the exam because it required a **technician's** licence, which she also did not have. But she wasn't discouraged. By the time the science fair arrived, she would have a different project put together entirely. This one would be focused on podcasts, which were quickly becoming the future of radio anyway.

Words: radio, academic, extra-curricular, remarkable, revolution, soothing, primary, secondary, signal, prompt, broadcast, attend, technician

Icon English Reading Success: Stage II

Passage 36: Science Fair

Write a summary of the passage using the repeated grammar rules and tenses that you can find in the passage.

_____
_____
_____
_____
_____
_____
_____
_____

Write 2 sentences containing **adjective clauses**.

_____
_____

Place a checkmark next to the sentences that contain an **adjective clause**.

____ The green vegetables are generally the ones that contain the most iron.
____ The school, which is home to the best football team in the country, is really quite prestigious.
____ I listen to pop music, which helps motivate me to exercise.
____ The problem with most cars is their declining reliability through the years.
____ My eyes followed the ball, which bounced all the way across the auditorium.
____ The magazine hires people who are culturally and artistically in-tune with the city.

Passage 36: Science Fair

NOTES

NOTES

Passage 37:
PE Class

Cameron's PE class currently occupied the school **gymnasium**, which was located in the front corner of the school next to the cafeteria. PE, which was also known as **Physical** Education, was the least favourite class of most students. The gym teacher, Coach Oliver, told the students they would each have to run one mile, and they would all be timed. People who were most **in-shape**, he told them, would be able to run a mile in less than ten minutes! Cameron was then determined to run as fast as he could.

One of the girls in Cameron's PE class was named Beth. Beth, whose sister had won last year's state **championship** for **cross-country** running, was not such a great runner herself. She seemed nervous and **stiff**, and when Cameron tried to comfort her, she grew angry and ignored him. He knew her rude behavior, which had been done in defense, had probably been a result of her **anxiety**, so he **shrugged** it off.

Cameron had bought new running shoes just a few weeks ago. Running, which most people were loath to do, had in fact become something of a hobby for Cameron, and he knew it was important to have great running shoes; shoes that have good arch-support tended to be better for a runner's feet and ankles.

All of the students followed Coach Oliver outside, and most were annoyed to have to leave the indoors. Coach Oliver grew tired of the grumbling, and told the class that he remembered the days when students actually enjoyed being outside, as opposed to staying inside and playing video games all day. Beth pointed out that everyone was complaining because it was raining, a comment which irritated Coach Oliver, and which he chose to ignore.

Coach Oliver set a timer, and the students began to run around the track. Not but two minutes later, Beth tripped over and fell, and immediately began crying. She had tripped over her shoelace, and her ankle, which she claimed had already begun to **swell**, was badly twisted. Coach Oliver took **pity** on Beth and let her sit inside while everyone else kept running. At the end of class, Cameron, who had run the mile in just under nine minutes, went over to Beth to see if she was ok. She winked at him and wiggled her ankle. She had faked the entire accident!

Words: physical, anxiety, gymnasium, championship, shrug, swell, stiff, pity, cross-country, in-shape

Icon English Reading Success: Stage II

Passage 37: PE Class

Write a summary of the passage using the repeated grammar rules and tenses that you can find in the passage.

_____
_____
_____
_____
_____
_____
_____
_____

*Write 3 sentences containing **adjective clauses**.*

_____
_____
_____

True or False?

____ Adjective clauses answer the question how many, what kind, or which one?
____ Adjective clauses contain a past participle and verb.
____ Adjective clauses begin with words like who, that, which, when, where, or why.

NOTES

NOTES

Passage 38: Geography Class

Ellen's **geography** class was at one o'clock. Having finished lunch early, she spent the rest of her break **wandering** around the library before the bell finally rang. She reached the classroom before any other students and, arriving early, saw her teacher eating the last of his sandwich while reading a book. Geography class was becoming one of her favourite classes, partly because her teacher was so great. Having earned a doctorate from UBC, Dr. Fields was very knowledgeable in multiple subjects.

The class went by quickly, and at the end he assigned everyone a **country** within the southern **hemisphere** to present on the next day. Ellen got back to her house later that afternoon and, determined to begin work on her project, she brewed a giant pot of coffee. She had been assigned Argentina, located on the **continent** of South America and **bordering** the countries Uruguay and Chile. The **official language** was Spanish, and being a rather large country, it had a **national population** of just over forty-three million people.

Exhausted from having worked all night, Ellen went to school the next day completely worn out. When geography class finally rolled around, she had regained her energy. Nervous and needing some encouragement, she went to the bathroom for a quick self-pep talk, and then rejoined her class. Her presentation went well, and assured by her own knowledge gained from studying up on Argentina the night before, she was able to include details about its colourful history and even the meaning of the **flag** of Argentina. After the class was over, Dr. Field congratulated her on her hard work. Relieved to be done with the presentation, Ellen treated herself to a chocolate bar from the vending machine.

Words: population, wander, country, flag, official, national, border, language, continent, hemisphere

Write a summary of the passage using the repeated grammar rules and tenses that you can find in the passage.

_____
_____
_____
_____
_____
_____
_____
_____

Place a checkmark next to the sentences that contain an **adverb clause deduction**.

____ Loving the show, she decided to create a painting depicting the main characters.
____ Tired from band practice, Ellen decided to go to bed early.
____ Lauren was excited to see her old friend again, and she knew she would have fun.
____ When Jacob got to the airport, he was upset to see a long line to check-in.
____ Knowing the consequences, we did it anyway.
____ Arriving at work, she felt a twinge of regret that she didn't just stay home.

Write 2 sentences that contain **adverb clause deductions**.

_____
_____

NOTES

NOTES

Passage 39: First Dance

Cameron and Ellen are going to the high school's annual Summer **Dance** together. Cameron picks Ellen up from her house at six-thirty in the evening. Cameron's car is immaculate, having been to a professional car cleaning service earlier that day. He wanted to impress Ellen with his tidiness. When they arrive at the high school, many students are already there. Everyone looks **formal** and **attractive**, having bought fancy clothes especially for the occasion.

When they go inside, Ellen sees Mr. George working as the school janitor. He is a kind, very tall man, and he waves at Ellen and Cameron before continuing with his duties. The **magnificent** gymnasium with a seat **capacity** of 3000 has been transformed into a **brilliant** wonderland for the event, which really delights Cameron and Ellen. Soon, they see Jen waving at them. Having worked in the same school senate committee with her, Ellen knows Jen well. Cameron knows Jen because they are neighbours. But, Jen brings her boyfriend along today, and he comes without **invitation**.

"We're setting up a karaoke machine!" Jen tells them. "Can either of you sing? It is not a **contest**, though."

"Not very well," says Ellen.

"Behold your prince and princess!" Suddenly, Jen's boyfriend speaks, and Jen just rolls her eyes.

Ellen can sing one song in French, but she knows not many people will understand the lyrics if she sings it at the dance, so she doesn't say anything.

"We're just here to dance," says Cameron honestly. He and Ellen like to dance, having danced at many school functions and friends' parties before, but never danced with each other.

Ellen and Cameron spend an hour or two dancing and joking with their school friends, and as the night is winding down, they share a **romantic** moment outside. Cameron likes to spend more time with Ellen, so he suggests they leave and see a movie together. She says yes, and tells him she would love to see the movie being shown in select theaters next week. Cameron is overjoyed!

Words: formal, attractive, magnificent, brilliant, capacity, contest, invitation, behold, romantic

Icon English Reading Success: Stage II

Passage 39: First Dance

Write a summary of the passage using the repeated grammar rules and tenses that you can find in the passage.

_____
_____
_____
_____
_____
_____
_____
_____

Rewrite the following sentences to include an **adjective clause deduction**.

1.) The people who work there get an annual raise.

_____

2.) The books that were published that year were best sellers.

_____

3.) I saw a lady who was carrying an umbrella.

_____

4.) A dog that tracks mud in the house will be punished.

_____

5.) The students who try their hardest will get good grades.

_____

Place a checkmark next to the sentences that contain an **adjective clause deduction**.

____ People wanting to go to the beach should wear sunscreen.
____ She wants something that contains less sugar.
____ The people hired last month will undergo training.
____ The bread made yesterday won't be as fresh as today's.
____ Who is the guy playing tennis with her?
____ People driving without insurance are breaking the law.
____ I talked to people who are taking the exam tomorrow.
____ My friends, used to certain luxuries, will not enjoy camping.

NOTES

NOTES

Passage 40: Drama Club

Alice's drama club was her favourite part of each school day. She was **perpetually** looking forward to the class because she knew she would be seeing her friends there. That day their drama instructor, Ms. Sara, sat them down. She told them she would be adapting a Shakespeare play into something more **modern**, and that she was hoping for some **input**.

"It could be done," said Alice's friend Jackie. "Would we be doing a **tragedy** or **comedy**?"

"The club does *Romeo and Juliet* **frequently**, but *A Midsummer Night's Dream* has never been done at this school before," said Ms. Sara. She was glancing around the room for reactions to this news, and wondered if her students thought the prospect of doing a new play might be exciting.

Alice liked acting no matter the material. She put up her hand. "We could try **improvising** a scene today, to see if it might work."

"That's a great idea!" said Ms. Sara. She began assigning various roles to the acting students, and once it was over, she went to the library to start printing copies of the script. All of the students waited in the drama room. They were whispering **animatedly**.

"Do you think it's possible we'll be doing this play?" asked one student. He was known to dislike Shakespeare because he thought of Shakespeare as a **playwright** who was totally irrelevant to the modern world. Jackie, however, had always considered Shakespeare to be inspiring, so she was looking forward to doing the play. When Ms. Sara came back with the scripts, she started handing them out. Alice was flipping through her script when Ms. Sara pulled her aside. She told Alice that she and everyone else had been very impressed with her last performance in the school play, and then said she was wondering if Alice might **audition** for this new play if they chose to **adapt** it.

"Not to worry," said Alice. "I will definitely be auditioning!"

Ms. Sara clapped her hands together. "All right, students, let's get to work! We are running out of time for today!"

Words: improvisation, animated, comedy, tragedy, frequent, modern, adapt, adaptation, playwright, input, perpetual, audition

Icon English Reading Success: Stage II

Passage 40: Drama Club

Write a summary of the passage using the repeated grammar rules and tenses that you can find in the passage.

_____
_____
_____
_____
_____
_____
_____
_____
_____

*Rewrite these sentences so that they include a **present participle**.*

I will drive him to school: _____
She goes for a run every morning: _____
We heard him sing: _____
They read books together: _____
The girls giggled at the joke: _____
Did you hear that?: _____

*Write a sentence that contains a **present participle**.*

_____

*Place a checkmark next to the **present participle**.*

____ helping   ____ biking
____ wants   ____ seeing
____ studies   ____ walking
____ paint   ____ looks
____ has

NOTES

NOTES

Passage 41:
Field Trip

Alice's class had left school for the day to go on a field trip. They had gone on two other field trips that year: one to the art museum, and the other to the city hall. Alice and her friend Jackie were excited to be going on the field trip because the teachers had **revealed** they were going to an Amish community. Amish people did not use any modern technology or electricity, and they lived their lives in a very **old-fashioned** way. Alice had gone to an Amish community when she was young, but she didn't remember much of it.

Their teachers had told them the Amish farm was far away and not set in a convenient **location**, so they should bring a snack or a book for the bus ride. Alice had brought a bag of grapes and a comic book, and her friend Jackie had brought a sandwich. Jackie had thought about bringing a **camera** on the trip, but in class the day before, the teachers had let them know that Amish people didn't like cameras or having their **photograph** taken, so they had been discouraged from bringing cameras. As **observers** of their community, the teachers had formulated a few rules for the students: they were not allowed to bring cameras or cell phones, and they had to be **polite** to the Amish folk.

Once they arrived at the Amish community, their teachers reminded them that all the rules would be enforced so they'd better behave. Then, the teachers took them to the various tents the Amish people had set up. One tent was devoted to the baked goods the Amish had made, and Alice and Jackie bought homemade butter. Prior to the field trip, Jackie had said Amish people were **abnormal**, but once they were actually there, Jackie saw how hardworking they really were! After the trip was over and everyone had gone back to the buses, Jackie and Alice discussed how kind the Amish people had been. They both decided they wanted to return and learn more about their unusual **community**.

Words: camera, polite, reveal, location, community, abnormal, observe, old-fashioned, photograph, enforce

Icon English Reading Success: Stage II

Passage 41: Field Trip

Write a summary of the passage using the repeated grammar rules and tenses that you can find in the passage.

_____
_____
_____
_____
_____
_____
_____
_____

Rewrite these sentences so that they include a **past participle**.

His eyes are looking red:
I cook him dinner:
She crashes the car:
The dog barks at the chicken :
We walk to the store together:
I work on my school project:

Write a sentence that contains a **past participle**.

_____

Place a checkmark next to the correct **past participle** of each **irregular verb**.

Bring:	____ brung	____ brought	____ bringed
Deal:	____ dealed	____ dealted	____ dealt
Drink:	____ drunk	____ drinked	____ drank
Swell:	____ swelled	____ swolled	____ swollen
Sink:	____ sinked	____ sank	____ sunk
Hang:	____ hanged	____ hung	____ hunged
Swim:	____ swum	____ swam	____ swimmed
Write:	____ wrote	____ writed	____ written

NOTES

NOTES

Passage 42:
Valentine's Day

John and Bella had been dating for one month, and Valentine's Day was approaching. To make sure it would be a perfect night, John had made reservations two weeks in **advance** for a fancy Italian restaurant **downtown**. He knew that in order to impress Bella, he would really have to step things up. On the evening of Valentine's Day, John had his **suit** hanging up so as to prevent it from **wrinkling**, and when he put it on, he sighed in relief. It wasn't wrinkled at all!

After he was dressed, he got on his computer in order to look up **directions** to the restaurant. To arrive on time, he would need to leave in approximately five minutes. John brushed his teeth so as to make sure his breath would not stink, and then left.

Meanwhile, Bella was at her apartment still getting ready. To ensure her hair would not be frizzy that night, she had washed it the day before. Her hair looked great, but her makeup was another story. She figured that in order to look her best she would have to pile on makeup, but to do that would not be true to herself, for she rarely wore makeup in the first place! Bella was nervous about the date, so she had a cup of tea and **consoled** herself with the thought that she did her best. To go on a date on Valentine's Day was a big deal, and she hoped everything would go well.

John arrived at Bella's house, and then they drove to the restaurant. He had picked her up a few minutes early so as to be sure they had plenty of time to drive to the restaurant and arrive on time, but it didn't matter—the restaurant was full, **despite** the fact that John had made a reservation! He could hardly **contain** his anger. The owner of the restaurant was embarrassed about the accident, so in order to **pacify** John he called a friend who owned another restaurant, and asked the manager there to set aside a table for John and Bella.

John and Bella went to the other restaurant, which was smaller and further away, but much less crowded and, as a result, far more intimate. They ended up having a great time! To everyone else, the restaurant might have seemed **dingy** and cramped. To them, however, it was a perfect place for a date on Valentine's Day.

Words: downtown, wrinkle, directions, contain, console, pacify, advance, suit, dingy, despite

Passage 42: Valentine's Day

Write a summary of the passage using the repeated grammar rules and tenses that you can find in the passage.

_____
_____
_____
_____
_____
_____
_____
_____

Complete these sentences:

In order to see the eclipse, _____

To most people, _____

In order to make the cheerleading team, _____

To her many fans, Sheila was _____

Write a sentence containing the phrase **so as to**.

_____

NOTES

NOTES

Passage 43:

Vancouver Aquarium

It was a beautiful day, and Mr. and Mrs. Martin were going to the Vancouver **Aquarium**. With no plans for the afternoon, they decided it was a perfect time to go there, for they had not been to the aquarium in years. Being a Monday afternoon, it was very empty. Without the crowds packed into the aquarium, it was easy to find parking close by, and they didn't have to wait in line!

Mr. Martin was excited to see the **aquatic** life, but Mrs. Martin wanted to see the **marine** animals. Without any time **constraints** to hold them back, they realized they were free to split up and do as they pleased! Mr. Martin went to the tropical **fish** section of the aquarium. Many different **species** of life could be found there, and he took his time studying each tank. With each new fish that he came across, his enthusiasm grew. The beauty of some of the fish **astonished** him; they seemed to **sparkle** as they swam.

Meanwhile, Mrs. Martin was outside watching the seals. The seals had a **diet comprised** mostly of fish. With so few people crowding around, Mrs. Martin was able to get a great view of the seal. Mrs. Martin read the plaque on the side of the tank, which described their natural **habitats**, and where in the world seals could be found. Without her glasses to better help her see, she had to squint to read the text. Suddenly, her phone rang, surprising her. Without the noise of large groups of people and **frantic** tourists walking around, which so often accompanied a trip to the aquarium, her phone had sounded quite loud! She answered it.

"Hey, where are you?" said her husband.

"I'm outside by the seals. Where are you?" she replied.

"I'm by the stingrays. Come inside!" he said.

Mrs. Martin met her husband inside, and together they went to view the stingrays. The employees allowed them to pet the stingrays after washing their hands. Afterwards, as they were walking back to their car, Mr. Martin smiled at his wife.

"Without you by my side, today would have been just another dull day," he told her.

Words: marine, aquatic, frantic, sparkle, constraint, habitat, diet, species, fish, comprise, astonish

Icon English Reading Success: Stage II

Passage 43: Vancouver Aquarium

Write a summary of the passage using the repeated grammar rules and tenses that you can find in the passage.

_____
_____
_____
_____
_____
_____
_____
_____

Complete the sentences:

Without her computer _____
With as much strength as she could muster, _____
Without sugar in the cabinet, _____
With all due respect _____
Without my glasses _____
With that in mind, _____
Without gas in her car _____
With the increase in rent, _____

NOTES

NOTES

Passage 44:
Plagiarism

At every school and even within businesses, plagiarism is a **serious offense**. Plagiarism is the act of **stealing** intellectual property, and the **consequences** are **dire**. John, who attends UBC, once knew a student who was **expelled** for plagiarizing. The student, whose name was Rick, was in John's economy class.

Over the weekend, a rumour was going around that Rick had plagiarized his last assignment. John wondered if the school board would have him expelled. If Rick was lucky, they would only have him suspended. When Rick arrived in class, the professor had him leave the classroom and go to the teacher's office, no doubt to await a scolding. John figured the professor would have Rick apologize for plagiarizing his essay, but Rick's consequences would be far worse.

Word about Rick's plagiarism had spread, and many people had come to disrespect Rick because of it. The other students in the class would rather have Rick be isolated than see themselves associated with a plagiarizer. But people who plagiarize only have themselves to blame. Stealing another person's work and passing it off as your own is not only **immoral**, but also **illegal**! If a person commits plagiarism, the school board will at the very least have that person put on academic probation. Their punishments for such rule-breaking are always very **harsh**.

Rick had been experiencing some personal problems at home. UBC has counselors to aid students struggling with personal matters, but Rick had never gone to speak with one of those counselors. John didn't know the details of what was troubling Rick, but he felt a little sorry for him regardless. Rick may have been having personal issues, but he clearly preferred to have his troubles kept private and have himself suffer in silence rather than seek help. It is a shame that Rick **resorted** to **copying** another person's work and turning it into the professor as his own instead of getting help with the assignment.

Words: consequence, dire, illegal, copy, steal, serious, harsh, expel, expulsion, immoral, resort, offense

Passage 44: Plagiarism

Write a summary of the passage using the repeated grammar rules and tenses that you can find in the passage.

_____
_____
_____
_____
_____
_____
_____
_____

Write a sentence that follows the **have + subject + to infinitive** format.

_____

Place a checkmark next to the sentences that follow the **have + subject + to infinitive** format.

    ____ He would only have himself to blame.
    ____ The principal will have the teachers focus on the perils of plagiarism.
    ____ I have so much to do today.
    ____ The dogs have veterinarians to care for them.
    ____ I have homework to finish.
    ____ We have a boat that needs cleaning.
    ____ I have read that book twenty times.

NOTES

NOTES

Passage 45:
Stanley Park

Cameron and Ellen go to Stanley Park. Cameron drives to Ellen's house to pick her up, and she notices his **bicycle hitched** to the back of the car. Her mom and dad have another bike sitting in their garage, and she wonders whether she should bring it. Cameron says not to worry about it. He is ok with simply walking today.

When they get to the park, it is quite busy. They search the map for a trail that will not be so crowded and then head into the woods. Soon after, they come across a park employee who is taping up a barrier, preventing them from traveling any further.

"Is the path closed today?" asks Cameron.

"Today, and all this week," the park employee replies. He tells them he will have the path groomed by the following week, but for now it is off-limits. Paths that have not been properly groomed can be **dangerous**, not to mention more difficult for hikers. Cameron seems disappointed, but Ellen has a plan building in her mind. She leads Cameron towards a path that ends by a **vast** lake. There, they find a cabin owned by a man renting canoes. Ellen asks the man if they can rent a canoe. To her **dismay**, he tells her that he can rent her one, but that the only canoe left has a broken oar! Luckily, he will have the oar fixed soon, and he just needs a few minutes to work on it.

Ellen opens up her backpack and takes out snacks. Cameron sees a hat inside her bag and pulls it out. At home, he has a hat very similar to the one he is currently holding. Ellen already knows this, and admits it was the reason she bought the hat in the first place; she liked his hat so much that she went and bought a similar one!

While they wait, they **gaze** at the clouds. Ellen and Cameron have imaginations superior to those of many children, and they see the shapes of various **birds** and **animals** in the clouds. One cloud **resembles** a **lion**, and another resembles a walrus. Finally, the oar on the canoe is fixed, and Ellen and Cameron take the boat onto the lake. They have opinions different from many people's when it comes to nature, but on one thing they can agree: spending time in the wilderness is a **wholesome** experience!

Words: resemble, lion, bicycle, dangerous, gaze, dismay, birds, animals, hitch, vast, wholesome

Passage 45: Stanley Park

Write a summary of the passage using the repeated grammar rules and tenses that you can find in the passage.

_____
_____
_____
_____
_____
_____
_____
_____

Write a sentence that follows the **have + object + adjective/participle** *format.*

_____

Place a checkmark next to the sentences that follow the **have + object + adjective/participle** *format.*

	____ I have a cat similar to yours.
	____ The librarians have dozens of books checked out every day.
	____ We have cars shinier than diamonds.
	____ He has enough homework for an entire classroom.
	____ I have cakes flavored vanilla, strawberry, and red velvet.
	____ She has opinions that are different from my own.
	____ You have grocery bags heavier than bricks.

NOTES

NOTES

Passage 46: Cooking Class

Alice Martin and her father Paul loved to bake, so they decided to take a cooking class together. Cooking can be a rewarding hobby, and they both wanted to improve their skills in the kitchen. The class assembled at the community centre. There were not many people in the class, but Alice and Paul were **optimistic**: fewer students meant more individual attention from the instructor!

"Creating new recipes can be difficult," their instructor told them. "But with dedication, it can also be exciting!"

Their instructor went on to tell them that being a great **chef** requires planning and patience. She handed out the **recipe** they would be trying out that day, and everyone got started. That night, they would be making a casserole. Alice and her father had never tried making a casserole, but they weren't discouraged.

"The worst thing that could happen would be burning it," Alice observed.

They began by cooking the noodles and setting the temperature on the **oven**. Preheating the oven is a crucial part of cooking. Alice let the noodles **simmer** on the stove while her father **chopped** tomatoes and onions. Once the noodles were cooked, Alice started making the sauce. Stirring the sauce repeatedly for five to ten minutes was vital to the recipe. That would allow the **ingredients** to properly mix.

At the end of the class, once everyone had finished making their casseroles, they got to taste their creations. Alice and her father's casserole was just ok. A better outcome, they decided, would have resulted from using higher quality ingredients. But they had to be thankful because the worst thing that could have happened would be burning or dropping the dish, which they were both glad not to have done! In the end, they were satisfied with their dedication and patience throughout the project, despite the dish not turning out the way they had hoped. **Plus**, as their cooking instructor reminded them, there was always next week!

Words: chef, recipe, simmer, oven, ingredients, stove, chop, optimistic, plus

Passage 46: Cooking Class

Write a summary of the passage using the repeated grammar rules and tenses that you can find in the passage.

_____
_____
_____
_____
_____
_____
_____
_____

Place a checkmark next to the sentences that use a **gerund** as a **subject/object**.

____ I find walking to be very therapeutic.
____ Painting has been her favorite hobby for nearly a decade.
____ We went swimming in the ocean but it was so cold!
____ Making friends can be difficult in new places.
____ She has been studying for three hours.
____ Working is a way to make ends meet.
____ She hates being late to school.
____ The company will be facing lawsuits.
____ Sleeping is important for brain health.

Write 2-3 sentences that contain a **gerund used as a subject/object**.

_____
_____
_____

NOTES

NOTES

Passage 47:
SAT Tutoring

The SATs were coming up, and Alice was nervous. Even more nervous, however, was Alice's mother. Mrs. Martin knew that if her daughter didn't do well on the SATs, she might have to take the exam a second time. Because of this worrying, she signed Alice up for SAT tutoring classes. The tutor was a man named Mr. Albert, and he told Alice on their very first tutoring **session** that if she studied, she was likely to pass the exam with flying colours! His reasoning was this: the more focused a person is when studying, the more **likely** they are to remember the material.

After a month of SAT tutoring, which had been a valuable learning **resource**, Alice felt prepared for the exam. However, when she and her mother left that morning, it was raining. Neither of them had expected the storm, and this was because the weather report had not mentioned a chance of rain the night before. If it had, they would have known to wear **waterproof** jackets! The rain also caused a delay in traffic, so when Alice arrived at the test centre, she was right on time but soaking wet! She was glad, then, that she and her mother had chosen to leave twenty minutes early. If they were any later, Alice would have had to take the test at a later date.

The SAT supervisors showed her to her seat, and she began the test. Time went by very quickly because the test seemed very easy to Alice. She knew she had her tutor to thank. Had a **lesser** teacher been her tutor, she would have had to study much more. But because he was such a great teacher, he had been able to teach the material in a very **effective**, **repetitive** manner! Alice looked up at the clock and was shocked: if the time was right, she only had ten minutes left to complete the test! She turned her attention back to the test, and **proceeded** to finish the final **portion**.

Words: lesser, waterproof, likely, effective, resource, proceed, portion, repetitive, supervisor, session

Passage 47: SAT Tutoring

Write a summary of the passage using the repeated grammar rules and tenses that you can find in the passage.

_____
_____
_____
_____
_____
_____
_____
_____

Place a checkmark next to the sentences that contain a **conditional**.

_____ She won't pass the test if she doesn't study.
_____ I was wondering if you could help me mow the lawn.
_____ If you have a car, getting around town is easy.
_____ Because she is the best employee, she will get a promotion next month.
_____ The more you practice, the better you will get.
_____ If you heat the frozen peas in the microwave, they will thaw more quickly.

Write your own **conditional** *sentence.*

_____

NOTES

NOTES

Passage 48:
Swim Lessons

Paul's boss had awarded him a bonus for his exceptional work at the hospital. He had thought about using the money to buy a fishing rod, but his wife gave him a different idea. Paul had never learned to swim, which was **ironic** considering his love of fishing. He reasoned that if he hadn't gotten the bonus, he wouldn't have had enough money to sign up for swim lessons. It helped too that his wife was so **supportive**. If she hadn't been so encouraging, he wouldn't have had the bravery to sign up. And, as he told his children many times, if you don't try, you cannot hope to improve.

The swim lessons were held in the morning. If they were held in the afternoon, it would be too crowded to swim. When he got to the pool, he saw swimmers doing **dives** into the **deep** end. Paul hoped their lessons would be on the **shallow** side of the pool. One of his biggest fears was **drowning**, and this was probably due to seeing the movie Titanic so many years ago. If he hadn't watched the movie he might have never developed a fear of learning to swim!

Paul was very surprised to see one of his coworkers, a **fellow** doctor named Bill, standing by the pool. Like Paul, Bill was already in his **swimsuit**, and he too looked nervous. Paul went to say hello, then confided in Bill that if Bill had told him he was signing up for the same swim lessons, Paul might not have been so reluctant to take the class in the first place! Bill laughed and told Paul that the feeling was **mutual**.

"If they don't clean the pool later today, maybe we won't have to come back next week!" he joked.

Words: mutual, dive, drown, shallow, deep, supportive, swimsuit, fellow, ironic

Passage 48: Swim Lessons

Write a summary of the passage using the repeated grammar rules and tenses that you can find in the passage.

_____
_____
_____
_____
_____
_____
_____
_____

*Place a checkmark next to the sentences that contain a **conditional**.*

____ If I had the time, I would have gone to the party with you.
____ He asked me if I could help him study for the exam.
____ I would travel the world if I had the money.
____ I gain weight when I eat too much.
____ Running gets easier if you do it more frequently.
____ We would have brought an umbrella if we knew it was going to rain.
____ I didn't know if he was mad at me.

*Write your own **conditional** sentence.*

_____

NOTES

NOTES

Passage 49:
Flying to Boston

Paul Martin was going to Boston with his family to visit his parents. He had not seen his parents in over a year and was anxious to see them again now that they were getting older. The Martin family got to the Vancouver airport at nine o'clock in the morning. His wife Lauren was antsy. She wished they had left earlier because the lines getting through **security** were sure to be long. After checking their bags and getting their tickets, they headed to the security line, where TSA agents announced rules and regulations, and told everyone in line to get out their **passports**.

Mr. Martin wished the line would move faster so that he could go to the café for his morning coffee. Behind him in line was John, who was grouchy. John wished he were able to stay home rather than travel to Boston. He had just started dating Bella and wanted to spend time with her. Ellen, meanwhile, was wishing she had brought a different book. She had begun reading it on the drive to the airport and found the book to be very boring.

After getting through security, they found their **gate**. The airplane that would carry them to Boston was being unloaded outside. Soon after, they began boarding. Alice hated flying, and wished they were travelling to Boston via train instead. At the start of every flight, flight attendants gave brief demonstrations on **airplane** safety and **precautions**, and this always made Alice nervous. She knew it was not likely that the plane would **crash**, but she still wished she would never have to go on an airplane again. Not only did they frighten her, but they made her **nauseous** too.

Once the plane had taken off, the flight **attendants** went down the **aisles** taking drink orders. Mr. Martin finally got his coffee, and Alice had a **carbonated** beverage to help with her upset stomach, though she wished she had thought to bring nausea medication instead.

Words: passport, security, airplane, aisle, gate, nauseous, boarding, precaution, attendant, crash, carbonated

Passage 49: Flying to Boston

Write a summary of the passage using the repeated grammar rules and tenses that you can find in the passage.

_____
_____
_____
_____
_____
_____
_____
_____

Write your own sentence in the **subjunctive mood (wish)**.

_____
_____

Complete the sentences:

I wish I had a car because then _____

She threw a coin in the fountain and _____

I didn't want to go to school today, and wished _____

He wishes he made the football team because then _____

NOTES

NOTES

Passage 50: Family Trip to Boston

They were one day into their trip to Boston, the **capital** of and most **populous** city in Massachusetts, and already the Martin family swore they would never return to Vancouver. Boston was beautiful, and they were smitten with the city. On their first day, all five of them took a tour of the Boston Tea Party ships. Their tour guide, a **native** Bostonian, suggested they go to the Boston Museum of Fine Arts while they were there, so they booked a tour for the following day. Ellen and Alice enjoyed the tour, but they hoped that they would be able to make a trip to Cambridge, Massachusetts to tour Harvard University, an Ivy League school **regarded** as one of the best in the country.

"If you're hungry," the tour guide told the Martin family, "there is a pizza place around the corner."

No one was hungry, so they continued to walk around the Tea Party ships. Alice and Ellen were getting anxious to leave and instead go see Harvard.

"If I lived here, I would definitely go to Harvard," Ellen **mumbled** to her sister.

Her father heard her and automatically whispered back, "And if you went to Harvard, we'd all be broke!" The family laughed at his joke, until their tour guide looked over at them **curiously**, and they all **stifled** their laughter.

Mrs. Martin was happy to be in Boston, but she was desperate to see New York City. She and her husband had visited New York City years back. She knew they would have scheduled a trip there if they had time, but they only had a few days to spend in Boston. And besides, she had already been to New York. If she had never been there before, she would have made the trip regardless of whether or not she had to go by herself!

"I **recommend** you keep up, unless you want to get left behind!" the **tour guide** called out to the Martin family. The rest of their tour group had already entered the Tea Party ships! The Martin family hurried inside to catch up with the rest of the group, **unaware** they had gotten so far behind. If they were any slower, their tour guide might leave them behind!

Words: populous, capital, tour guide, stifle, regard, native, unaware, recommend, curious, mumble

Icon English Reading Success: Stage II

Passage 50: Family Trip to Boston

Write a summary of the passage using the repeated grammar rules and tenses that you can find in the passage.

_____
_____
_____
_____
_____
_____
_____

Write a sentence in the **subjunctive mood (conditional)**.

_____

Write a sentence in the **subjunctive mood (imaginational)**.

_____

Place a checkmark next to sentences that are written in the **subjunctive mood** *(conditional or imaginational).*

   ____ You should only eat if you're hungry.
   ____ If I were president, every month would have a Halloween!
   ____ You should keep up the pace or else you'll get left behind.
   ____ I would have taken your advice if I knew it was worth something.
   ____ I want to be a bird. I would fly every day.
   ____ She said I won't get into a good university if I don't try harder.

Passage 50: Family Trip to Boston

NOTES

NOTES

www.ingramcontent.com/pod-product-compliance
Lightning Source LLC
Chambersburg PA
CBHW061753290426
44108CB00029B/2979